Farming and society since 1700 in the barony of Carbury, Co. Kildare

T0348855

Maynooth Studies in Local History

SERIES EDITOR Michael Potterton

The six volumes in the MSLH series for 2024 cover a broad chronological and geographical canvas across four provinces, focusing variously on people, places, families, communities and events. It begins with an unlikely search for Vikings in the north-west of Ireland, where the evidence is more compelling than most people realize. Further south, in Carrick-on-Shannon, we trace the fortunes of the St George family from the Plantation of Leitrim through to the decades after the Famine. From Carrick we continue south to Ballymurray in Roscommon and its Quaker community (1717–1848), including their relationship with the Croftons of Mote Park. Further south still, in 1701 Jacobite Patrick Hurly of Moughna, Co. Clare, was at the centre of a 'sham robbery' of gold and jewellery worth about €500,000 in today's money. Unlike Hurly, Mary Mercer was renowned for her charitable endeavours, including the establishment of a shelter for orphaned girls in Dublin three hundred years ago in 1724. Finally, the last volume in this year's crop examines the evolution of the resilient farming community at Carbury in Co. Kildare.

* * *

Raymond Gillespie passed away after a very short illness on 8 February 2024. He had established the Maynooth Studies in Local History (MSLH) series with Irish Academic Press in 1995, from which time he served as series editor for a remarkable 27 years and 153 volumes. Taking over those editorial reins in 2021, my trepidation was tempered by the knowledge that Raymond agreed to remain as an advisor. True to his word, he continued to recommend contributors, provide peer-review, mentor first-time authors (and series editors) and give sound advice. Shoes that seemed big to fill in 2021 just got a lot bigger.

Maynooth Studies in Local History: Number 171

Farming and society since 1700 in the barony of Carbury, Co. Kildare

Lesley Whiteside

FOUR COURTS PRESS

Set in 11.5pt on 13.5pt Bembo by
Carrigboy Typesetting Services for
FOUR COURTS PRESS LTD
7 Malpas Street, Dublin 8, Ireland
www.fourcourtspress.ie
and in North America for
FOUR COURTS PRESS
c/o IPG, 814 N Franklin Street, Chicago, IL 60610

ISBN 978-1-80151-134-6

Printed in Ireland
by Sprint Books, Dublin

Contents

Acknowledgments   6
Introduction   7
1 Carbury before 1700   11
2 The eighteenth century: within the Colley estate   15
3 The eighteenth century: outside the Colley estate   28
4 The nineteenth century: before and after the Great Famine   43
5 The nineteenth century: land reform   62
6 The twentieth century: organization and growth   71
Notes   81
Abbreviations   81
Index   89

FIGURES

1   Carbury Castle   12
2   Map of barony of Carbury   13
3   Newberry Hall   17
4   Coolavacoose   26
5   Ballinderry House   29
6   Grange Castle   33
7   Kilglass House   42
8   Clonkeen School   50
9   Coonagh House   57
10 Ballindoolin House   70
11 Ardkill House   79

Acknowledgments

I am grateful to David Clarke and Rachel Clarke, residents of the barony of Carbury, for drawing maps and illustrations for this book; to Andrew Whiteside for general assistance with the text and for the cover photograph; and to Michael Potterton, series editor, for his wisdom and encouragement. Whenever I sought information within the barony, I received generous and invaluable help.

Introduction

This study examines the barony of Carbury's long-established
reputation as an unusually stable and prosperous farming
community of Co. Kildare. Previously, historians have concentrated
on the early history of Carbury, while Karina Holton contributed
to the *Irish villages* volume a chapter that extended to the twentieth
century.[1] While there are many publications on farming and society in
Ireland, none has concentrated on Carbury. W.E. Vaughan's *Landlords
and tenants in mid-Victorian Ireland* has an extensive bibliography,[2]
which includes local studies in other counties, and *Kildare history and
society* has several chapters relevant to Carbury.[3]

Formerly, an historian might have been deterred from a study of
farming and society in Carbury by the difficulty of accessing sources.
The early records of most Irish families have been lost[4] and it is
difficult, therefore, to represent the patterns of landownership and
the lines of succession in the barony in the sixteenth and seventeenth
centuries. Henry Colley's acquisition of lands from the 1530s can be
traced through the fiants. Another family, the Tyrrells, were living
at Grange in the fifteenth century,[5] where it is believed Sir John built
Grange Castle in 1460. Descended from Hugh Tyrrell, the Anglo-
Norman baron of Castleknock, whose son Gerald became lord of
Fertullagh, Co. Westmeath, the Tyrrells were originally tenants of
another Anglo-Norman family, the Berminghams. They became
and remained owners until Bobby Tyrrell made it over to the state
in 1988. The Ballinderry branch of the family retains a large archive
showing the farming activity of the Tyrrells as they spread across the
barony.

In recent years, however, estate papers of the eighteenth and
nineteenth centuries of the Palmers of Rahan, the Bors and the
Tyrrells of Ballindoolin and the Tyrrells of Grange, Carrick and
Ballinderry have become available at OMARC (BAL) in Castletown
House and the Ballinderry Papers can be consulted in Ballinderry
House by arrangement with the owner. These archives contain

valuable material, which extends to other estates in the barony and warrants academic investigation.

Papers of the Colley estate have long been available as the Harberton Papers (T2954) in the Public Record Office of Northern Ireland but they consist mostly of letters and associated papers and lack key items, such as estate rentals and farm accounts. For the barony of Carbury, a comprehensive survey of the Colley estate, completed in 1744 by Moses Byrn, offers an unparalleled insight into its farming community. It can readily be compared with the information in Richard Griffith's 1854 valuation. With the survey in hand, it is possible to walk the land and envisage how the tenant of the time farmed his holding.

There are few extant records for the rest of the barony, in which the pattern of landholding was complex, and none of the owners of the numerous estates has left a comparable archive. The limited consideration of these is selective and is intended to be indicative. (The destruction in an 1888 fire of most of the archives of the large More O'Ferrall estate at Balyna is a serious loss.)

The limited survival of records and Anglican predominance in landownership from the Reformation until the early twentieth century lead to an Anglican emphasis in this study. If, however, one combines these estate papers with farm records kept by Roman Catholic tenant farmers, the Boylans (National Library of Ireland P.7214)[6] and the Duggans (John C. Duggan, *250 years at Highfield*),[7] it is possible to build a picture of their position in the farming community. Farm records kept by Anglican tenants, the Holts of Coolavacoose (Maynooth University, Centre for the Study of Historic Irish Houses and Estates, Holt Papers), show that they treated their farm labourers equally, irrespective of religious affiliation, while a search of the Registry of Deeds revealed no difference in the treatment of Roman Catholic tenants, such as the Boylans and the Duggans, from that of their Anglican neighbours. Another relatively recent asset is the online availability of deeds from the Registry of Deeds. These give an understanding of landownership, tenancy, land use, marriage settlements and mortgages and they offer insights into the need to provide for children other than the heir, the indebtedness of the landowning class and the frequency with which mortgage defaults led to the loss of land.

One of the appealing aspects of this study is that it deals not with the great and famous but with the ordinary farming people of Carbury and the 'small' people of society, whose names have virtually disappeared. There was no truly famous figure in the barony after the seventeenth century, the most illustrious probably being members of the More O'Ferrall family of Balyna, who maintained a large estate and distinguished themselves in the service of foreign armies in Europe. Richard More O'Ferrall was a long-serving MP, sat on the 1833 royal commission to investigate the condition of the poor in Ireland, was an adviser to the Catholic University and attained several significant government posts. While the family's position as large landlords was important, it did not dominate the area in the same way as the dukes of Leinster or the Conollys of Castletown did in east Kildare.

In 1700 a small proportion of the population was literate and many who could read and write did so at a basic level. Only the educated few wrote letters, diaries or journals, which would fill out the picture of farming life in Carbury but none has been found. The 'small' people do, however, make cameo appearances, including the servant, Denis Kelly, who witnessed a lease by Lewis Moore of lands in Cadamstown to Patrick Dempsey in 1737,[8] 'John Field, a deserted child', baptized in Carbury church in 1838,[9] and Elizabeth Logan, employed in 1810 on the Holt farm at Coolavacoose.[10]

Many of those who lived before the civil registration of births, marriages and deaths became compulsory in 1864 are not recorded in any published document. Although Anglican and Quaker records fill some gaps and there are Roman Catholic parishes, such as Balyna and Carbury, from which earlier registers survive, much information is missing.[11] While some Church of Ireland parishes have records from the seventeenth and eighteenth centuries, those of Carbury date only from 1804–5.

As this is a study of farming and society in Carbury, the discussion of political issues is kept to a minimum. Some of these have been addressed by recent historians such as Terence Dooley and Ciarán Reilly.[12] Every effort has been made to standardize the spelling of names of people and places. Until the twentieth century, however, it was very variable and it has proved impossible in some cases to ascertain what was intended. Until the 1830s, measurements of land are given in Irish plantation acres, as was the practice of the time. Subsequently the references are to English statute acres, reflecting the transition then being officially made. (An Irish acre was equivalent to 1.62 statute acres.) In 2024 readers may think in hectares, converting one acre to 0.6555 hectares.

1. Carbury before 1700

Any study of the farming community of Carbury, in north-west Kildare, must start with a consideration of the landscape. Situated in the central lowlands, the underlying soil is carboniferous limestone, covered with glacial moraine and scattered peat bogs. These soils, combined with a moist cool-temperate climate, provide favourable conditions for grassland and tillage. It has long been famous, however, as a grazing region, described in 1744 as being 'in the heart of a richly fertile country'.[1] The topography is reflected in many of the Irish-origin place-names, particularly in townlands such as Clonkeen, derived from *cluain* (dry meadow, surrounded by bog or water); Garrisker (*Gearr eiscir*), from the esker which crosses the parish of Balyna; and Kinnafad (*Ceann átha fada*), 'the head of the long ford', on the River Boyne. Other place-names such as Ballinderry (*Baile an Doire*), 'the townland of the oak grove', indicate that the area was once widely planted with trees and the place-names Kilglass, Killinagh and Kilmore may also indicate woods rather than churches, as there is no evidence of a church at any of these locations.

A brief introduction to the history of Carbury before 1700 is necessary: Carbury Castle, still prominent in the landscape (fig. 1), was built by the Bermingham family, which in time wavered in its loyalty to the crown and joined forces with the O'Connors of Offaly. In 1500 the Berminghams still held most of their lands but the earls of Kildare were extending their influence in the area and threatening the king's authority. When Silken Thomas, the tenth earl, rebelled in 1534, Henry VIII had him executed and was determined to quell all resistance in Co. Kildare. The lands of Sir Walter Delahide, one of the earl's allies, were confiscated, those in Carbury being leased to Captain Henry Colley. Colley's lease gave him the site of the castle or manor, lands of Ballyhagan, Ballyvane, Carbury, Clonkeen, Clonmeen, Coolavacoose, Derryart, Kilmore and Kishavanna.[2]

Government attempts to achieve control of the country relied on military outposts and establishing English and Scottish settlers on

1. Carbury Castle, the medieval stronghold of the barony (by Rachel Clarke)

lands near a manor house, with a church, market and local courts. (As Henry VIII had broken with Rome in 1534 and established the Church of England, according to the principle of *cuius regio eius religio*, the Church of Ireland was established as the church of the state.) Settlements were isolated and vulnerable to attack from the Irish and although Colley was knighted and greatly augmented his lands, it was an achievement to pass his estate to his sons. Its early division after his death reduced its importance in the area. Potentially one of the great estates of Kildare, had it remained intact, the Colleys would have been more likely to continue to reside there. Instead, George, his older son, inherited the Edenderry estate, which ultimately passed through the female line to the absentee marquess of Downshire. Henry, Sir Henry's younger son, inherited the manor of Castle Carbury, Ardkill and Collinstown and the estate passed down his direct line.

While landlords such as Henry Colley were granted their land in the sixteenth century, it was only in the next century that an estate system evolved in Ireland. The more secure landlords, supported by the rents of their tenants, initiated agrarian improvements, 'a reorganized pattern of farms, fields and roads was introduced and the large residences of the landowning class, each surrounded by a landscaped park, became a principal feature of the landscape'.[3] In poorer or more disturbed areas, however, little development happened. Given the turmoil of the seventeenth century in the Carbury area, improvements on the Colley estate were limited and

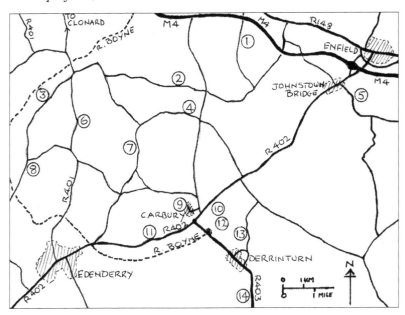

2. Map of the barony of Carbury. 1 Balyna House; 2 Kilglass House; 3 Rahan House; 4 Ballinderry House; 5 Metcalf Park; 6 Ballindoolin House; 7 Williamstown House; 8 Grange Castle; 9 Carbury Castle and old church; 10 Ardkill House; 11 Coolavacoose; 12 Newberry Hall; 13 Coonagh House; 14 Drummin House (by David Clarke)

the Colleys were not leaders of agrarian developments. The castle and demesne never recovered after being attacked in the 1641–2 rebellion and much of the small Anglican population fled permanently.

A lengthy period of turmoil followed the rebellion and Oliver Cromwell's war in Ireland was devastating. His 1652 settlement was the first in a series of confiscations and grants of lands, in which supporters, first of Charles I, then of Cromwell himself, subsequently of Charles II, James II and William III lost or gained property and wealth. The complicated circumstances of many changes of ownership are illustrated by the case of John King, who gained land in Carbury under Charles II. He was not an English officer, being the eldest son of Sir Robert King of Boyle Abbey, Co. Roscommon. He had served under Cromwell but after his regiment was disbanded in 1653 he devoted his energies to increasing his landholdings by buying up indentures from English soldiers. Having become disillusioned with the Cromwellian regime, he worked for years for the Restoration, upon which he was created 1st Baron Kingston. He was, however, forced to surrender some of the lands he had bought, in compensation for which he received lands in Kildare and Limerick. Likewise, Henry (Viscount) Moore, who had lands in Carbury, as a Royalist soldier, paid a large amount to retain his estates under the 1652 Act of Settlement but was rehabilitated after the Restoration and was created earl of Drogheda. These families, having large estates in other parts of Ireland, never lived in Carbury and their chief influence lay in their choice of Anglican tenants.

By the late seventeenth century, the Colley estate had been divided (possibly on the basis of townlands) into fewer than twenty-five tenancies. If the estate was divided on such lines, there were fifteen townlands of one hundred acres or more which would have constituted good-sized farms, while other townlands might have been combined to make a viable holding, as at Longridge and Coolgreany. All 250 acres of Coonagh (fig. 2) were leased to Henry Salmon in 1691[4] and the Grattans were already established at Clonmeen, where Simon Grattan died in 1697.[5] The Grattans were not a typical Carbury family, in that they were not landowners but were gentry, who became prominent in church, medical and legal circles in the eighteenth century, both in Dublin and in the Carbury-Edenderry area. Dr John Grattan (born in 1713) was a medical practitioner in Edenderry and was succeeded by his son Thomas and grandson John. As gentry, they formed a middle ground between the aristocracy and the average tenant farmer on the estate. While it would have suited Henry Colley to have his estate farmed by a small number of large tenants, he must have realized that none of them could manage a big holding without considerable help and that sub-letting was inevitable. It was not long before this process began.

2. The eighteenth century: within the Colley estate

The Colley family retained its position in society despite the damage inflicted on the estate during the turbulent years of the seventeenth century. Henry inherited it in 1700 but his marriage in 1719 to Lady Mary Hamilton, daughter of the sixth earl of Abercorn, encouraged him to pursue interests beyond the barony of Carbury. He became MP for Strabane in 1723, shortly before his death. His younger brother, Richard, inherited the Wesley family estates in Co. Meath and changed his name to Wesley (Wellesley) following the death of his cousin Garret Wesley, whose mother was a Colley. He was given the title of Baron Mornington.[1] The change of name, a common occurrence on the inheritance of an estate, was a small price to pay for a younger son whose fortunes were so greatly changed.

Henry Colley's death at a young age in 1724, followed quickly by that of his baby son Henry, was a disaster for the Colley estate. His infant daughters, Elizabeth and Mary, who inherited it, were brought up by their mother. It is unlikely that Lady Colley had much affection for the dilapidated castle that became her home when she married Henry. During her long widowhood, she spent much time in London and Dublin, where she was active in social circles. In the 1730s, she was renting a house in Grosvenor Square, London, where her neighbours included the dukes of Norfolk and Cumberland.

It is an indication of the lowly status of women, even in landowning families, that although she was the eldest child, Elizabeth's existence has been almost totally forgotten, while Mary appears in Burke's *Peerage* as Viscountess Harberton, by virtue of her marriage to Arthur Pomeroy. In those days it was difficult for women to manage an estate even if it was well run and in good condition. Very little is known about the estate in these years and it was only when Elizabeth and Mary approached adulthood that they assumed responsibility for it. Mary, born in 1723, had not even come of age when they commissioned a survey of their lands. Their chief motivation was probably a desire to assess the value of the estate and to divide it between them in advance of either of them marrying. They must also have observed that their fellow landlords had become the agents of agricultural progress, introducing new methods, improved breeds, new crops and rotations with clover and turnips, and planting orchards and hardwood trees, and perhaps they recognized their need for guidance.

Byrn's report and maps,[2] completed in 1744, are of great interest. He was more like an agricultural consultant than a land surveyor, in that his maps are elementary. Sarah Bendall's comprehensive *Dictionary of land surveyors and local map makers of Great Britain and Ireland* does not list any other work by him.[3] (An unspecified Byrne collaborated with Garrett Hogan on a map of Mountrath in 1735.)[4] It is likely that he had at his disposal existing maps and a rental, so that the maps he produced were included only to elucidate his report. He made no attempt to convey the physical geography of the area, apart from rivers, and his representations of towns, individual large houses and other buildings are whimsical. His workmanlike presentation relied heavily on the written report. This was in contrast to John Rocque's surveys of the estates of the earls of Kildare. Described by John Andrews as 'some of the most remarkable estate surveys ever made in Ireland',[5] Rocque used self-explanatory pictographs and colour illustration to convey much of what Byrn described in his report. The opulent bindings of Rocque's maps suggests that their chief purpose was aesthetic while Byrn's work, in a plain binding, was utilitarian.

Byrn's examination of the estate, townland by townland, showed that there were about fifty divisions by this time. (There are ninety-three townlands and eleven civil parishes in the barony of Carbury.) A townland, typically covering an area of 100 to 500 acres, was always subject to enlargement and division.[6] Townland boundaries are generally marked by streams, ditches, banks and hedges. Their mapping, begun in the sixteenth century, was important to successive governments in facilitating the confiscation and apportionment of lands in the context of plantation and war. The names, with a few changes, remain in use in the twenty-first century.

Byrn registered that the Colleys had orchards, gardens and meadows near the castle and farmed part of the demesne, while

3. Newberry Hall, built by Arthur Pomeroy to replace Carbury Castle (by Rachel Clarke)

leasing some of its fields and all the rest of the estate. He suggested that they should repair the castle and that they could increase rents if they improved the land by building double ditches and planting them with good hedges, by liming and manuring the land and by appropriate ploughing. He offered recommendations specific to each holding and his rent figures gave the rate per acre which he considered each was worth, offering a valuation rather than a statement of the existing rents. (His estimated rental came to £2,963 1s. 10¼d.)

Starting with Carbury Hill, he described it as 'a most profitable sheep walk' and the land there 'so fertile that it would bear onions and leeks'. He proclaimed it as the most pleasant hill in Ireland, which should never be divided, as it was a lovely place for people to walk and it offered a view of the four provinces. He was up to date with contemporary developments of demesnes, in which fields were reordered into grid patterns and the mansion house sat within a symmetrical landscape, with avenues radiating from the centre, all designed to draw the eye to the house, impress the viewer with the extent of the landscape and manifest the landlord's wealth and status. Accordingly, he proposed that the ladies build two new avenues, one going to the Dublin road, the other running south to the ringforts, in one of which they should erect a gazebo. The use of the word 'gazebo' shows him to be a follower of fashion, as this term for a garden pavilion did not come into use until the middle of the eighteenth century. His further recommendation was to 'raise Castle Carbury demesne house another storey high and fix windows regular in the front thereof. [Then] the place would look as grand and spacious as in the whole province of Leinster'. Byrn must have been an optimist because the castle and grounds were not in good order. There was a vast contrast between its appearance and the demesne at Carton, Co. Kildare or at Stradbally, Co. Laois, which had formal structures, widespread planting of trees and orchards, kitchen garden, flower garden, bowling green, statuary and topiary. Moreover, landowners were increasingly abandoning the defensive castle and tower house in favour of the restrained elegance of Georgian mansions. The Colleys were then in no position to restore the castle and it was twenty years later, after Mary's marriage to Arthur Pomeroy, that Newberry Hall provided the estate with its own Palladian mansion (fig. 3).

There is a contradiction in Byrn's aspirations for the village of Carbury because, on the one hand, he stressed its identity as a manorial village, with its castle, church, court leet and court baron, biannual fairs and weekly market, while, on the other, he refers to it as a town 'fit for a manufactory and place of trade, being a great throughfare to and from Dublin to several parts of the kingdom, in the heart of a good country'. Despite his hopes, the village was not affluent. There were only four houses and four cabins, all thatched and most of them built of stone, a brewhouse, malthouse, chair house, barn and stable, which were all in need of repair. One large house had three chimneys, indicating that the builder had been well-off, but decay had set in. In proposing that two fields could be spared from the demesne, a new town built and 'inhabitants planted therein', Byrn had in mind the estate towns which had been emerging since the 1720s and was perhaps envisaging one with market square and wide streets as in Blessington, Co. Wicklow or Summerhill, Co. Meath. If this was his aim, he was sadly deluded.

Byrn showed an awareness of the legalities of the estate. When entering the 7s. 6d. payable each year as chief rent on Kilrathmurry and Clonard Bridge, he pointed out that the royalties of the entire village belonged to the Colley family and that all its residents

> are obliged to do suit and service to the court leets and court barons of the manor of Carbury as often as they are lawfully summoned and now the seneschal of the Misses Colley, who are ladies of the manor, should never neglect to summon the inhabitants of Kilrathmurry to Carbury court.

Reporting that 'James Moore of Balyna commenced a law suit for …
part of Tanderagee', he commented that 'Lady Mary Colley attached
said Mr Moore at law and got the better of him, for which … the
Misses Colley and their tenants quietly and peaceably enjoy the land'.
Byrn was perhaps distracted by the legal issues at Tanderagee, for he
omitted to list the tenants and assess their holdings. He was, however,
thorough in his survey of almost all the holdings. He repeatedly
stated that a good farm had to be 'convenient to manure, fire, water
and market' and needed a good farmhouse. He suggested that the old
castle 'with good strong walls' at Clonkeen, held by Patrick Coffey,
should be repaired as it would then be 'a commodious useful house
for the farmer'; that 'the Misses Colley should give timber to roof
it and beams … for the loft, and oblige the tenant to slate the castle,
which will be as cheap as thatch'. He further noted that there was a
dwelling house, barn, stable, cow house and three cabins on the land,
all needing repair. In Ardkill, where John Payne held 378 acres, he
noted an 'old castle, formerly the seat of the son and heir of Henry
Colley', a dwelling house, brew house, barn, stable and cow house, all
in poor condition but which, if repaired, 'would be a very fit seat for
a gentleman'. He also listed an orchard, garden, calf park and three
cottiers' houses. Undoubtedly, the garden was a kitchen garden to
produce vegetables and fruit for the family, rather than an ornamental
garden, which was then the preserve of the rich.

Byrn favoured 'regular fields' and in many of his reports
recommended the reinforcement or construction of wide and high
ditches and the planting of good native hedges, clearly grasping their
importance in providing shelter and secure boundaries. He showed an
understanding of the agrarian technological innovations of his time,
repeatedly urging the liming, manuring and draining of land and
the reclamation of bog. Recognizing that the Carbury tenants were
primarily cattle and sheep farmers and that the quality of pasturage
was, therefore, vital, his suggestions were aimed at improving
underfoot conditions and shelter for livestock and better growing
conditions for tillage, as all farmers grew crops such as wheat, barley
and oats, potatoes and vegetables. (He made several mentions of the
suitability of 'black cattle', probably referring to the ancient Kerry
breed or some other derivative from the Celtic Shorthorn, which,
due to its small stature, did less damage on damp soils.)

He specially praised farms such as those of Samuel Sale and John 'Cremor' (probably Cramer) at Coolcor. At the former, he saw a good farmer's house and outhouses, 'good warm ditches' well planted with whitethorn and crab and a kitchen garden; at the latter, buildings 'all in right good order'. At Jonathan Scott's in Kishavanna he commended two houses, malt houses, stables, barns and cow houses, nine cottiers' houses, mostly good cabins, land divided by good ditches planted with crab and whitethorn, an orchard, well planted and bearing good fruit, and a kitchen garden, both well kept and surrounded by ditches with hedges 'kept clipped and trained to grow thick'. On wetter sections, as on Widow Stevenson's in Kishavanna, he specified that the ditches should be planted with 'quicks, sallies and osiers to drain and shelter the land'.

His reference to warm ditches is in contrast to cold ditches which he found on some of the low lands, particularly in part of Clonkeen south of the River Boyne, which was constantly flooded by water from the bog. He added that this section of Henry du Boe's holding 'very much wants to be drained' and that it was 'very bare and bleak for want of the improvements and shelter'. Christopher Dowdall's adjoining holding came in for sharp criticism, as the land was 'much worn by being every year planted up and bearing corn' and because he had not repaired an old mill. Byrn remarked that 'the mill, if built, would turn to great benefit for the tenant; being convenient to Edenderry town, [it] would get good trade'. Similarly, at Haggard, although there were two houses with adequate farm buildings and the land was 'well divided into regular fields, with good ditches, well planted with whitethorn and crab', he described the land as 'very much worn, being constantly every year kept ploughed and bearing corn, [which] extracted the substance of the land'.

Byrn gave much consideration to the problems of bogland, considering that at Haggard it could be made 'pasturable', while 'a skilful person' should be employed by the Misses Colley to cut drains in Carbury bog. He effectively wrote off the bog at Ballyhagan, on the basis that it was 'useless to the tenant because it cannot be drained'. He indicated that he had walked the good land with the tenant and had shown him how it could be divided into more fields. Presumably Byrn also impressed upon him that all the buildings needed to be repaired, as 'the present house is a clay wall now tumbling down [and] wants to be rebuilt with a good stone wall, lime and sand'.

Among the few holdings that met with Byrn's approval, the best was at Clonmeen and Rinaghan, where John and Robert Grattan farmed 811 acres as undertenants of Richard Wesley Colley. There, Byrn registered his approval of good houses, barns, stables, chair houses, cottiers' cabins and large orchards. At Windmill, where John Brereton and his undertenants farmed 180 acres, he commended good houses and outhouses and two half-acre orchards, both sheltered by many ash trees and bearing good fruit. Despite the depredations of time, one can still see evidence of eighteenth-century tree planting on the estates and on the lands of stronger tenants such as these but the apples faded from the countryside.

At Kilmore, where seventy-six acres were farmed by Christopher Dowdall as undertenant of Thomas Coates, Byrn approved of a good *new* house, barn, stable and cow house, a gristmill for grinding corn, a tuck mill for processing woollen cloth and two kilns for burning lime, 'the walls of all said houses built with stone, lime and sand in good repair', two cottiers' houses and a well-grown orchard. The rent for the land was £43 but an additional rent of £40 was paid for the mills there and the mill at Windmill. At Freagh, where Francis Duggan held fifty-nine acres, he noted a dwelling house, barn, small orchard, kitchen garden and gooseberry garden, all 'out of repair'. He also observed the walls and chimneys of a good farmer's house, which would have potential if it were finished. His view here extended beyond the agricultural potential of the estate, as he wrote enthusiastically about 'a rich lead mine' on the land, which, if it had flourished, would ultimately have damaged the agricultural economy. His note that 'if kept in repair,' the associated smelt house and wash house 'will be useful to whatever tenant takes the land' indicates that Duggan had a short lease, as was the case with many of the tenants.

Byrn did not refer to the nature of leases but it is known that some tenants had only a yearly tenancy and no written lease. Their rents could be increased but the tenancy did not expire at the end of the year and the law presumed that it continued unchanged. The tenants' capacity to make improvements depended not only on the nature of their tenancy but also on relations with the landowner. On the Colley estate, many tenants felt sufficiently confident to build good houses and haggards, to plant trees and to drain the land. There were many changes in tenancies in the first quarter of the eighteenth century and the example of Coonagh illustrates the complexity of the situation on the Colley estate. Henry Salmon's 1691 lease was for his life and that of his son John and of Henry Hurst, son of Elias Hurst, thread maker of Dublin.[7] As Salmon was variously described as a gentleman 'of Dublin' and 'of Coonagh', it is unclear whether he ever farmed the land himself. After Henry Salmon's death, John assigned the land to Henry Hurst of Drummin for the lives of both of them, noting that the land was then in the possession of William Fayle, Patrick Flinn, Hugh Scully and Ann Salmon, Henry's widow.[8] In 1744 Henry Hurst was listed as the tenant, with the land divided between his sub-tenants William Neill and James Boylan. The evolution of the farms at Coonagh demonstrates the degree of change in landholding at the time and there were many other cases of tenants assigning leases or subletting. It is also clear that some lessees and assignees did not intend to farm the land themselves but viewed it as a mere investment.

Byrn's report showed that many of the tenants on the Colley estate in the 1740s had undertenants but he named only a few. It is probable that some of those undertenants took over as the main lessees when the previous tenants sold their interest or died. While there had been a concerted effort at the time of the Tudor settlement to ensure that tenants were Anglican, by the 1740s there were Roman Catholic tenants and there is nothing to suggest that they were treated differently from their Anglican neighbours. Excluding the demesne itself, some of which was estimated at 16s. and 18s. per acre, the average rent of land was a little more than 13s. per acre. It ranged, according to the quality of the land, from 8s. per acre at Ford House to 13s. in parts of Ardkill and Kishavanna.

It is impossible to give a complete picture of the estate in 1744 because the listed reports on Ballyvane, Derrinturn, Derryart and Oldcourt, including Coolavacoose, are missing. There were far more people involved than those named in Byrn's report but it is impossible to estimate the number of subtenants, farm labourers and associated tradesmen, such as blacksmiths and millers. On the Grattans' large farm, for instance, much labour was required, most of it provided by their unnamed subtenants. While there were frequent changes of tenant, a solid core of stable tenant farmers was evolving that was to prove the basis of the farming community through ensuing centuries.

The Colleys had been apprised of the necessary improvements but apart from specifications in some leases for planting trees, ditches and hedges, there is little evidence that they initiated them. It is unknown whether tenants saw Byrn's report (some of them may have been illiterate) but one can suggest that pro-active tenants who were apprised of it used it as a template for improving their land. However inactive the Colley family was, it seems that the estate and its tenants were swept up in a wave of rural development and optimism. National production rose to meet expanded market demand and, aided by improved communication links, exports grew. These advances fostered a new sense of security in the Irish countryside. The former plantation mindset of defence and pacification at last gave way to a positive belief in progress and former settler families discernibly developed an Irish identity. It was against this background that landowners built fine new houses. In 1747, when Mary married Arthur Pomeroy, the two sisters were described as being 'of London' but they still spent some time in the castle. Within a few years, however, Pomeroy built Newberry Hall on a nearby part of the estate and the old castle became a roofless ruin. After their marriage, he became a party to all of Mary's legal transactions and a deed of partition, by which the estate was approximately halved, was concluded in 1752.[9] Elizabeth was still unmarried in 1759. By 1764 she had married Joshua Glover of Kingston-upon-Thames and he became a party to her deeds. Glover, a surgeon, died in 1783 and Elizabeth lived for a further thirty years. As she was childless, she left her estate to her nephew, the Revd John Pomeroy, and the Colley estate was again one.[10]

Although there is little evidence of the Misses Colley acting on Byrn's report, it may have encouraged them to establish a charter school in the village in 1747, in the hope of improving education and employment prospects in Carbury. It was one of some sixty schools established by the Incorporated Society in Dublin for Promoting (English) Protestant Schools in Ireland, with the objective of training children, both Anglican and Roman Catholic, for useful employment so they would not be a financial burden on the parishes.[11] Most of the schools failed miserably, for they were badly run and offered little education. Their proselytizing did not win over 'popish' children to the established church, rather it left a legacy of hostility to Protestant education.

The school did nothing to relieve the depressed state of the village. With the castle's decay, it is safe to assume that the old church, lying beneath it, was also in disrepair. (One wall of the small square church still stands inside the old graveyard on Carbury Hill.) In 1771 Elizabeth Colley and Joshua Glover granted George Tyrrell of Dunfierth and William Cave of Oldcourt, churchwardens, a site for a new Anglican church and churchyard.[12] Consecrated on 27 September 1775, it did improve the village. The Colleys, however, soon ceased to live in Carbury, where their influence was much reduced.[13] Arthur Pomeroy was raised to the peerage as Lord Harberton in 1783 but the estate retained the name of Colley. Local people continued to walk up Carbury Hill to enjoy the views and their pleasure was in time enhanced by the planting of trees along the path from the village. The future of Carbury church did not depend on the Colley family but on a small number of faithful farming families, some of whom are still parishioners in the twenty-first century. In an agrarian society such as Carbury, continuity on the land was vital for the sustainability of the parish, whether the parishioners were landowners or tenants. While Anglicans had a new church in which to worship, Roman Catholics were still restrained from church building and had to wait until the relaxation of the penal laws in the nineteenth century permitted several new churches in the barony.

As to the charter school, in 1772 the Incorporated Society awarded a premium to the master and mistress, John Jackson and his wife, 'in consideration of their extraordinary great care of the children and school'.[14] A mere ten years later, Sir Jeremiah Fitzpatrick, the inspector-general of prisons, produced a devastating report that led to the dismissal of the Jacksons,[15] but frequent complaints continued. Although the school continued to provide apprentices both locally and in Dublin,[16] in 1796 the master, Stephen Sparks, was fined because some pupils had run away.[17] Lord Harberton sat on the committee but he and the other members were oblivious to the dreadful conditions in the school and failed to comprehend that it provoked the Roman Catholic majority. It was not surprising that the charter schools were unpopular in local society and the use of some of them as military bases during the 1798 rebellion further exposed them to opprobrium.

This provocation to local insurgents was not needed in the case of Carbury, where disturbances broke out before the 1798 rebellion.[18] A first attack on the school was foiled but the school was burned down in May 1798, the children were dispersed and the building was offered for use by the military.[19] Commendably, the Revd Charles Palmer, vicar of Carbury, went to the school immediately after the attack and arranged to accommodate the children locally until the Incorporated Society could provide for them. There was no attempt to re-establish the school and its closure may have had little impact locally. Its land was subsequently granted by Harberton as glebe land and for a parish school but the field where the school was located is still called 'the charter field'.[20]

The charter school was not the only place in Carbury to suffer during the 1798 rebellion, for there were subsequently a few claims for damages. Most of the claims were modest: John Jackson, a farmer at Carbury, claimed £89 for the loss of cattle and hay, while Arthur Smith of Carbury claimed £24 and William Smith of Drehid claimed £35 for damage to their houses, and others claimed for the loss of cattle, clothes and furniture. The largest claim was for £848, by Dr Richard Grattan at Drummin, for his house being burnt, with the loss of books and a bookcase. There was an extraordinarily large claim by Sparks, the school master, for furniture, clothes, cattle and silver, totalling £648.[21]

On 11 July 1798 Thomas Tyrrell of Grange commanded the local cavalry against the rebels. The centuries-old loyalism of the Tyrrells was probably the cause of an attack on Garrett Tyrrell's house at Ballinderry that day and of other attacks on Tyrrell homes in the centuries to follow.[22] The rebels went on to Newberry Hall, where they killed two dairy maids, Mary and Esther Grattan. Retribution followed swiftly when Lieut. George Gough and his men drove off the rebels, killing fourteen of them. Five men were convicted of murder and four of them were hanged at the scene of the crime. This may have discouraged further insurgency, for disorder in Carbury village abated after July 1798. The eighteenth century ended badly, particularly for Anglicans in Carbury, as they were reminded of the terror of the 1640s and knew that, although the rebellion caused relatively little damage in their locality, the Anglican community in

4. Coolavacoose, an eighteenth-century tenant farmhouse, still lived in
by the Holt family (by Rachel Clarke)

some parts of Kildare suffered more. The prospect of further attacks
loomed but diminished in ensuing years.

The events of 1798 did not detract from the considerable progress
made within the Irish farming community in the second half of
the eighteenth century, during which landowners and tenants both
thrived. Locally, as Patrick Duffy writes, the growth was remarkably
good, because the estate system was 'grounded in a strong and
enduring tenant farming community' whose prosperity 'was reflected
in eighteenth-century food surpluses and the early emergence of
two-storeyed thatched houses on well-managed extensive farm
units, some of which survive to the present day'.[23] The houses of two
tenant families, the Holts at Coolavacoose (fig. 4) and the Clarkes at
Kishavanna, are prime examples, although the thatch has long been
replaced. It is difficult, however, to date such houses as the method of

construction and materials used changed little between 1740 and 1840. While these families remain in their houses, making alterations as necessary, the more prosperous and ambitious Grattans had given up their lands at Clonmeen and Rinaghan and taken a lease of Drummin, where they had built a large Georgian house and gradually acquired a considerable holding.

Neither is it easy to date the substantial Georgian farmhouses, such as Brookville, Kinnafad and Oldcourt, which tenants built on the Colley estate, as the standard designs prevailed for many years. Most of these are plain, symmetrical two-storey buildings, with the rounded door opening and fanlight and large sash windows typical of early Georgian rural architecture. They are solid but not showy, probably reflecting the mindset of those who built them. Coonagh is a 'pretty' house, believed to have been modelled on nearby Newberry and built *c.*1770, while Oldcourt is a distinctive building, given a slated roof from the beginning. On the Colley estate, Taylor's 1783 map of Kildare marked only Newberry and Oldcourt as having slated roofs,[24] and the transition from thatch on newbuilds was slow and gradual. Thatched roofs were gradually replaced on existing houses, as at Coonagh, which was slated in the 1830s.

The owner of Coonagh, John Boylan, was known as 'John the Rich'. When he died in 1797, he held from a number of landlords farms totalling about 1,500 acres, which he divided between his three sons: Clonkeeran to James, Martinstown to Edward, and Coonagh, Drehid and Parsonstown to Patrick. He also left generous pecuniary legacies to his grandchildren and charitable bequests to the local parishes.[25] In rejecting the principle of primogeniture, presumably in favour of fairness, John Boylan broke up what could have been a major farm holding in the nineteenth century. While the next generation was financially comfortable, none could have been nicknamed 'the rich'. Few of his fellow tenants would have described themselves as 'rich' but as agriculture expanded and became more profitable during the years after Byrn's survey, many were living in good houses on improved land and it is easy to understand that ensuing generations of strong tenants would aspire to own their own farm.

3. The eighteenth century: outside the Colley estate

While the Colley estate had survived the seventeenth century, its multiple traumas had a major effect on the rest of the barony. It is difficult to trace the movement of people on the land but there were serious upheavals during changes of ownership and as families fled for safety. Instability in landownership persisted until the end of the century brought a period of peace under William and Mary but even then the consequences of the wars were felt. For instance, the lands of John Bellew, baron of Duleek, in Kildare, Louth and Meath had been forfeited due to his support of James II during the Williamite war. His son Richard eventually recovered the family estate but amassed such great debts in the process that he was forced to sell some of his land, as at Drehid, Dysart and Calfstown in 1710.[1] In contrast to the Bellews, another Roman Catholic family, the O'Mores of Balyna, were fortunate to retain their lands considering that Rory and Lewis O'More had been leaders of the 1641–2 rebellion. In time, the estate passed through marriage to Richard O'Ferrall of Co. Longford and the family adopted the name of More O'Ferrall.

Some who had gained lands in the seventeenth century disposed of them. Among these were the Lords FitzHarding of Berehaven, English royalist politicians and soldiers, who were not interested in the Irish lands they had been granted and gradually disposed of them. Thus, in the 1690s, the fourth viscount conveyed 600 acres in Rahan to George Colley of Edenderry by a perpetually renewable lease, which in effect made him the owner.[2] The security given by a perpetual lease enabled the creation of the Palmer estate at Rahan after Charles Palmer, youngest son of Thomas Palmer of Killaskillen, Co. Meath, and Mary Colley, inherited it from his mother's brother, Charles Colley of Rahan. This was the most significant development to affect the wider farming community in the barony in the eighteenth century, because the family became resident and

5. Ballinderry House, one of several Tyrrell houses in the barony (by Rachel Clarke)

active both on the farm and in the community, in contrast to their relatives, the Colleys, who became absentee landlords. The fortuitous way in which the estate was formed is revealed in the 1742 will of Thomas Palmer of Killaskillen, Co. Meath. He had married Mary, daughter of George Colley, in 1708 and they had nine children. Having left one shilling each to his son George on the grounds that he was already provided for by Mary's brother, Dudley Colley, to his son Dudley, as he had been provided for by Thomas Palmer's brother, John Palmer, and to his daughter Susanna, 'she being well married', he bequeathed a yellow in-calf heifer to his daughter, Judith; and his 'holding and chattels' to his daughters Mary, Anne and Margaret, and his two other sons, John and Charles, 'to be equally divided between them'.[3] This was an unusually egalitarian document, giving equal weight to daughters and sons, but it posed potential problems for the five children who inherited the bulk of his estate. The generosity of two uncles relieved Palmer of the need for his eldest son George or his second son Dudley to inherit. Although this was a frequent occurrence, it was extraordinary that it happened again to Palmer's family after his death, when his youngest son Charles inherited from Mary's other brother Charles.

The Palmer estate was centred on Carrick and Rahan, where Rahan House was built on landscaped grounds in a farm of 350 acres. The Palmers enjoyed a good reputation as landlords, farmers and employers. Their involvement in the barony was deepened when the Revd Charles Palmer, Charles Palmer's son, was appointed vicar of Carbury in 1796, a ministry he exercised until 1840, living in his own house for lack of a vicarage. The family lived in the barony much longer than their Colley cousins, the last being Charles Colley Palmer, who died in 1927 at the age of 82. The long continuation of the Palmer estate illustrates the benefits of a perpetual lease in giving security on the land. Ballinderry has likewise passed down through the Tyrrell family since William Tyrrell of Kilrainy obtained a perpetual lease from another non-resident landlord, Josiah Hort, archbishop of Tuam, in 1743 (fig. 5).[4]

Although inheritance was the norm, ownership of land sometimes was achieved when a mortgage was not paid off, in which case the mortgagee became the landowner. Mortgages were well-established ways of raising money and were used by landowners and tenants alike. They proved a good investment for the mortgagee and were frequently the first step in acquiring land. They were, however, dangerous for the landowner, who was frequently tempted by their easy availability but might overreach himself, default on payments and lose his land when the mortgagee foreclosed. The predominance of Dublin mortgagees and lessees is not only indicative of the flow of money in the city but also suggests a close link between financiers, investors and the legal practitioners who drew up mortgages and leases. Most of these legal documents were not only perfected in Dublin but were also signed and witnessed in the city, often in an inn. For instance, Walter Bermingham's 1718 mortgage of a moiety of Grange and of lands at Kinnafad to Thomas Motley, a Dublin skinner, was signed and witnessed at the Tavern in Smock Alley.[5] The letting, subletting or assignment of leases to Dubliners was deleterious to farming as many leases were taken as an investment and proved short-lived.

Dublin newspapers frequently carried advertisements for land to let, under headings such as 'near Clonard bridge' or 'on the main road to Birr'. The absence of a more specific geographical description suggests that Dubliners were familiar with the barony of Carbury as a potential place in which to invest.[6] Such lessees did not live in Carbury but rather sublet their holdings to undertenants, who lived on the land. Other outsiders, such as the Bors, converted an initial tenancy to ownership. Humphrey Bor appears to have been a London lawyer, who moved to Co. Meath about 1690 and became a farmer near Kinnegad. While he obtained a lease of 408 acres in Carrick and Ballindoolin through his marriage to Deborah Mills in 1722,[7] his successors became owners of the land and gradually increased their holding.

Another exception to the trend of tenancy as a mere investment was the small Quaker community that arrived in the barony at the beginning of the eighteenth century, for they did intend to live on and farm the land. They constituted a new element in Carbury society, when they moved north from the farming settlement which William Barcroft established at Ballymorane, on the other side of Edenderry, in 1673. His story is an interesting twist on an English Cromwellian soldier in Ireland: having become a Quaker, he settled in Co. Armagh until he was jailed for refusing to pay tithes. (As Dissenters, the Quakers were opposed to paying tithes or taking oaths in a court of justice and, like their Roman Catholic neighbours, suffered under the penal laws. They were widely persecuted and were sometimes subjected to higher rents than their neighbours.) Barcroft first moved to Co. Laois but a second jail term for non-payment of tithes led him to move to Ballymorane. Initially the Quakers there concentrated on sheep and cattle farming but many of them fled persecution during the Williamite war, when their property was damaged and their livestock was taken by the Jacobites. When a second wave of Quaker settlers came in 1692, they diversified into milling and woollen manufacture and employed about a thousand people in the woollen mill in Edenderry. They built a Quaker meeting house in the town in 1707–8, entered general trade there and dominated its business life for the next century. The Quakers were known for their strong social conscience and were active in providing relief for the poor in the decades before and during the Great Famine.

Among the Quakers who moved as farmers to Carbury was Barcroft's son John, who obtained a lease of 290 acres in Ardkill in 1711. His family did not stay there long, preferring, like many other Quakers, to live in the Quaker village at Ballitore.[8] Other Quakers were determined to stay, among them William Smith and his neighbour, Thomas Jackson, who in 1710 received from Richard Bellew two of the first leases listed in the Registry of Deeds.[9] (Although there are extant leases before 1708, they are only easily traceable after the establishment of the registry in that year.) While Quakers, such as the Smiths and the Jacksons, intermarried, the community was so small that most families ultimately moved to another part of Ireland, emigrated or married local Anglicans. The Smiths and the Jacksons continue through the female line in the Gallies and the Douglases, demonstrating the continuity of settlement in Carbury.[10]

Although emigration does not seem to have been a major option in eighteenth-century Carbury, Quakers were more inclined towards it and William Penn's colony in Pennsylvania was especially attractive to them.[11] Ann, daughter of William and Judith Smith of Drehid, was an early emigrant to Pennsylvania with her husband, Thomas Jackson.[12] Another early emigrant was Benjamin Chandley, who left about 1703, aged approximately 18. (It was probably significant that he was the eighth child.) He became a successful clockmaker in Pennsylvania and his son a distinguished compass maker. Benjamin's father was the miller at Kilmore mill and part of the family later moved to Ballitore.

A study of farming and society in Carbury must also consider wider aspects of life at the time, including health and education. Until the twentieth-century advances in medicine, inoculation and vaccination, even the common cold could lead to death, especially in a family that was poorly fed and living in a damp cottage with no running water and limited hygiene. Wealth provided little protection, however, and diseases such as tuberculosis, diphtheria, scarlet fever and measles killed children and adults in large mansions *and* humble cottages. Child mortality at all levels of society was so high that farming couples hoped to raise to adulthood *one* son who would take over the land. Succession on a farm, whether owned or leased, was compromised by the lack of a son to inherit. Occasional glimpses of efforts to ensure succession in such a case are afforded by deeds and wills. For instance, a childless farmer might leave his land to a nephew or cousin, reserving only a life interest to his widow or he might make a will bequeathing everything to his widow but adding a reversion to a third party of his choice in the event of her remarrying.[13]

Couples who raised many children had to consider provision for them all. Many farms could support only one family, in which case the oldest son generally inherited, while younger sons had to acquire land elsewhere or find a different occupation. The disappearance of

6. Grange Castle, built in the fifteenth century, where the Tyrrells originally settled in Carbury (by Rachel Clarke)

farming sons from a barony can sometimes be explained by marriage or inheritance elsewhere in Ireland. For those with education and status, possibilities included ordination to the priesthood or a commission in the army; in less-educated families, which made up the majority of the population, younger sons might seek employment on an estate, take up one of the many trades that were useful in the community or move to Dublin as tradesmen. If there was enough land, a farmer, whether landowner or tenant, might divide it among two or more sons. An example of this subdivision is seen within the Tyrrell family. In 1772 Thomas Tyrrell, who had a perpetual lease at Grange, made over his title to part of Grange and several other townlands to his son Joseph.[14] Two years later, he conveyed to his sons, William and Thomas Tyrrell the younger, his interest in another 180 acres in Grange, with the contents of the house, the farm animals, wool and the crops in the ground and in storage (fig. 6).[15] Sons who gained from such a subdivision often built a new house on their land.

The farming community throughout Carbury began to prosper in the more settled atmosphere of eighteenth-century Ireland but it is difficult to assess the extent to which the landlords generated agricultural improvements and the building of good farmhouses and outbuildings on their land. One agent of improvement came from the Quakers' emphasis on sheep farming, which stimulated woollen manufacture in Edenderry and encouraged other farmers to build up flocks for wool rather than to concentrate on beef cattle. Prominent among these farmers were the Sales, Colley tenants who prospered by selling their wool to the French military for the manufacture of uniforms needed in wars against England. The French had previously bought wool from England, which had a famous centuries-old woollen industry, but repeated conflicts from 1778 encouraged them to source wool from Ireland and Carbury farmers seized their opportunity.

Life revolved around livestock and food. In order to make a farm profitable, the farmer had to provide food for the expanding population of Ireland, estimated as three million in 1700 and between four and five million in 1800. Of these, about 60,000 lived in Dublin in 1700, a figure that more than trebled during the eighteenth century. In the days before refrigeration, freshness was vital so Carbury's proximity to Dublin gave its farmers ample opportunity to supply the capital with many of its dietary requirements. The most profitable product was beef, in the production of which Carbury excelled.

Carbury cattle and sheep farmers sourced young animals in western counties in spring and autumn and fattened them for the trade, a system that continued into the twentieth century.[16] There was a strong tradition of breeding on the rich grasslands of east Galway and Roscommon in particular. Young cattle and lambs would then be delivered to a collection point, usually Ballinasloe, where they were met by the drovers, who walked them (often cattle and sheep together) to Carbury over several days. This was a very slow process, as it was important not to stress the animals. There were designated stopping points along the route where they could rest and feed and they might cover only seven or eight miles (11 or 12km) a day. Similarly, when ready for market, the animals were walked slowly to Dublin, whether they were destined for consumption there or were to be shipped live to England. Once they had landed at a port such as Liverpool or Holyhead, they could be walked as far as London. On the way, they might encounter cattle, sheep and even geese being walked to the capital from the north of England and Wales, all going slowly because everyone knew that a hurried animal would not produce good meat and the buyer would therefore not offer a good price.

Such practice is alien to the modern mind but this and every other part of farming was slow until the advent of the combustion engine and twentieth-century mechanization. As long as farmers used only hand tools, it remained labour-intensive. The tools were simple, some like spades, reaping hooks and sickles, were made by a local blacksmith but easily maintained by the farm workmen; others, like the flail, were made on the farm, using two sticks tied together with willow stems or stretched animal skin. The plough and the harrow were the only tools that required frequent attention by the blacksmith, who alone could steel the coulter or provide new pins for it and the harrow. The blacksmith also had regular work shoeing working horses for the farm.

Until refrigeration was introduced, Carbury was too far from Dublin to be a dairying area, though farmers invariably kept dairy cows to supply the house. Middle-sized farms employed a small number of labourers throughout the year, the women managing the dairy and poultry. At harvest time, more workers were required and casual labourers were employed. For instance, many workers were needed to harvest a field of barley: after it was cut with a reaping hook, binders came behind and tied it into bundles, seven or eight bundles being made into stooks. It was then carted to the yard and made into a stack. The lengthy process of threshing might take the whole winter to finish.

While not strictly a farming activity, the turf harvest was also intensive and men would work for weeks on the bog, cutting by hand and 'footing' into heaps, leaving it to dry before drawing it home. Likewise, the potato harvest was also a lengthy process and every able-bodied person, adult and child, in the family was pressed into service. Small to medium-sized farms needed neighbourly cooperation and the *meitheal* was an established way of bringing in all this harvest. Men and boys went from farm to farm, being fed by the women and enjoying an easy camaraderie during the hard work and there was usually a hearty celebration at harvest home. Early in the eighteenth century, the potato harvest was not a major feature. Potatoes, originally introduced to Ireland about 1590, had spread from being a crop of gentry kitchen gardens to widespread planting by all classes. What began as an addition to the diet of the poor was, by 1750, becoming the staple diet of labourers and small farmers. Richard Twiss, an Englishman who published an account of his 1775 tour of Ireland, was amazed at the universal use of potatoes at the tables of the Irish gentry, where a dish appeared at every meal. Significantly, however, he remarked that the poor ate potatoes 'all year round without tasting bread or meat', except perhaps at Christmas, when the diet might be extended if the men had made enough from their labour or the women from their spinning.[17] The potato had many advantages in that it grew well in Irish conditions, was nutritious both for humans and for animals and was a valuable crop for clearing ground. On the other hand, it had a limited storage period and was increasingly vulnerable to disease. The introduction of new varieties, predominantly 'the Apple' (edible throughout the year) and 'the Cup', had some resistance but the labourers' increasing reliance on potatoes bode ill for the future.

In the rural landscape of Carbury, there was a network of buildings related to farming. Among the most important were mills, built by landlords to serve their estates. Under the traditional 'milling soke' system, the tenants had to have their grain ground at these mills and paid a toll (usually in kind). While windmills with wooden bases had long been used in Ireland, they were gradually being replaced by stone windmills, with large-diameter sails producing more power to work up to four sets of millstones. The windmill which gave its name to a townland on the Colley estate has totally disappeared but there are considerable remains at Windmill Cross, east of Derrinturn, and the stone walls of a cylindrical windmill at Johnstown Bridge endure. According to the inscription, it was built by Lewis Moore of Balyna in 1714. Windmills fell into disuse, their decline accelerating after the Napoleonic Wars ended in 1815, at which time cereal milling became less profitable.

Water-powered mills, already in use for many centuries, became more popular in the eighteenth century. Although they demanded a high standard of engineering and extensive construction, they scored over windmills as they had a more reliable source of power. Most watermills were situated not *on* a river but on constructed mill races. Where the supply of water was not assured, as was often the case in summertime, the mill pond was a vital asset in storing water overnight and releasing it during the day. Watermills were scattered across the barony of Carbury, some of them marked on Alexander Taylor's 1783 map of Kildare. Most were grain mills but at Kilglass, he entered a bleach mill and an unspecified mill. The bleach mill must have been used for bleaching linen and it is possible to envisage an accompanying bleach green on the map. As weaving was almost entirely a cottage industry, the second building was perhaps a scutching mill, from which the fabric was distributed to local weavers, who sent the fabric back for bleaching. There is still a 'flax field' there but almost nothing is known about the cultivation of flax or the production of linen in Carbury. The nineteenth-century establishment of a scutch mill at Carbury proves that flax was still grown locally but its short lifespan suggests that flax was finally eclipsed by the cattle and sheep trade.[18] It is likely that the linen trade in the barony was associated with the Quaker community, which was at its strongest in the early years of the eighteenth century.

Although the linen industry in Carbury was small and the cattle and sheep trade was predominant, eighteenth-century farmers produced a large amount of grain for sale as well as for their own requirements,

as is shown in accounts of flour sent by land carriage to Dublin in the
1770s. In 1777–8, Edward Daniel of Clonkeen sent 1,136 cwt and in
the following year, Henry Mather, also of Clonkeen, sent 1,038 cwt,
while John Jackson of Carbury sent 162 cwt.[19] By 1800 thousands
of watermills were operating throughout Ireland, the majority for
corn and flour milling but they were also used for such processes as
threshing, sawing and stone crushing and the manufacture of paper,
textiles, beer, whisky and agricultural tools. As the number of mills
proliferated, they grew in size and were a dominant feature of the
rural landscape, as, for example, Ballyonan corn mill, which still
stands but it is in a very poor state. Very few working mills survive
in Ireland.

Forges were another common feature of the countryside, as there
was a constant demand for the blacksmith to make and repair farm
implements and shoe horses. Handsome stone-built forges were
often located at crossroads but others were set up in a farm building
converted for the purpose. Forges gradually lost their significance
as farmers began to work with tractors rather than horses, bought
manufactured farm machinery and, after rural electrification, acquired
arc welders to carry out repairs in the farmyard. The heritage of the
forge is still preserved on farms in the surviving name of 'the forge
field'.

There were probably lime kilns, commonly called 'lime houses', in
many townlands. These were often well-built, arched stone structures
but there are few survivors across the country. While lime was used
for building mortar and render and for limewash on walls, from the
farmer's point of view its most important use was as a fertilizer on the
land. Lime kilns later fell into disrepair when farmers began to use
artificial fertilizers and cement replaced lime in the building trade.

Forges and lime kilns contributed to the loss of woodland in
early modern Ireland but there was widespread planting in private
woodlands during the eighteenth century, a good proportion of which
was oak. As has been noted, ash shelter belts were commonly planted
round good farmhouses and, as the eighteenth century progressed,
avenues to big houses were increasingly lined with imported species,
such as beech, lime and horse chestnut. Tree planting on a larger
scale was encouraged by the Dublin Society, founded in 1731 to
foster the economic and cultural life of Ireland. From the 1740s, it

awarded prizes for planting and issued a growing list of species which it considered suitable. Among the trees it was recommending in the 1760s were Scots pine and larch and it later added exotic species such as Lebanese cedar. These plantations, mostly in demesne woods, further depleted the ancient woodland that had once covered much of the area. Quarrying could also be destructive of farmland and woodland. Taylor's map marks only one quarry, at Carrick, but it is likely that farmers did their own small-scale quarrying as they needed stone, gravel or sand.

An oddity in the landscape was the dovecote, 'dove house' or 'pigeon house' as it was often called. Much less common in Carbury than in the south-east of the country, where it was found mostly on demesnes and large farms, it housed birds which provided a source of fresh meat in winter, eggs and manure. A survival from medieval Ireland, it was typically a round stone structure with a domed roof, resembling a giant beehive but more elaborate octagonal brick dovecotes were built in the seventeenth century. It is unknown how long the dovecotes at Grange, Kinnafad and Rahan, noted in the Civil Survey of 1654, survived and there may have been others in the barony.[20]

In 1700 the barony of Carbury was traversed by a network of paths and tracks on which roads were eventually built. (The earliest routes mostly led to medieval ecclesiastical centres such as Clonard or to sites of fairs.) Whether for work, trade, church attendance or social purposes, people had to walk or use horse power. Existing roads and tracks twisted and turned to avoid geological hazards and the many bogs (the actual bog being traversed by plank roads). During the century, improvements were made to existing roads and the rate of road construction increased under the aegis of the grand juries. With better technological aids, the new roads cut straight lines across the country, largely disregarding gradients and the existing pattern of communications. This can be seen, for instance, on Taylor's map, in the straight road crossing the north of the barony from Johnstown Bridge to Clonard. For the most part, however, daily farming life in the area was little improved by this new road. Likewise, the much-vaunted prospects promised to farmers by the builders of the Grand Canal, at the south of the barony, and the later Royal Canal at its north, never materialized.

As on the Colley estate, the prosperity of the eighteenth century encouraged the building of better farmhouses. In 1700 most of the old castles had been abandoned and the families who had lived in them had moved away or were living in modest dwellings. Farmhouses in the barony were typical of the local Irish vernacular style. Built with locally sourced stone or cob and thatched with local oaten or wheaten straw, these single-storey thatched cottages, often covered with limewash or rough harl, were well integrated into their environment. Increased prosperity encouraged the replacement or extension of these houses and the building of sturdy outhouses. Some of these improvements were modest, achieved by adding rooms in linear fashion by incorporating sheds or byres or by adding an upper storey. Others produced new large stone houses, some built by landowners, many by middle-sized tenant farmers.

The new houses signified the development of a distinct social hierarchy within the farming community. The earliest of these was at Gorteen, which later came to be called Metcalf(e) Park. Built in the early decades of the century, it is an impressive three-storey, five-bay gentleman's residence with rubble-stone walls and slate roof, square-headed sash windows, round-headed front door and decorative fanlight typical of Georgian country houses. Detached four-bay rubble-stone outbuildings were erected on opposite sides of a courtyard which, with the addition of a gate and gate lodge, constituted a considerable set of buildings. The National Inventory of Architectural Heritage captured the importance of such an agricultural complex in its 2002 report, stating that 'the survival of this group is of social importance, representing an intact eighteenth-century farm, which contributed to the historical development of the village of Johnstown Bridge whilst historically providing employment to the local community'.[21]

There is scarcely any written evidence about the building of such houses. It is, therefore, not proven that Metcalf Park was built by Joseph Medcalf. (An illustration of the evolution of names is provided by this family, whose name in the original lease to the lands of Gorteen was 'Medcalf', who later became known as 'Metcalf' and later still, had a final 'e' added.) In 1708 Joseph Medcalf of Dunfierth obtained from Lord Bellew a lease of 216 acres of Gorteen and Ballyboy, for his life, that of his wife Alice and of Thomas Barcroft of

Parsonstown. Presumably Joseph and Alice were young and recently married in 1708, as their own names were two of those specified. Lessees usually inserted the names of children in a lease for lives, so as to prolong it as far as possible. Nearly thirty years later, in 1736, Joseph obtained a new lease, in which he substituted the lives of his three sons.[22] Joseph and his family firmly established themselves at Gorteen and at some stage changed its name to Metcalf Park so it is almost certain that he built the house and courtyard.

Metcalf Park and Williamstown, built in the 1760s for Adam Williams, agent for the Downshire estate, stand out in contrast to almost every house in the barony in being named for the family rather than the townland. This unmistakable claim to status within the community was so strong in the case of Williams that the townland's name changed from Moorestown[23] to Williamstown. In 1770 he commissioned a map 'of the several parks' of his demesne. It shows only an outline of the eighteen divisions of the 172 acres but the names alone give an indication of his societal aspirations. Division 9 covers the 'mansion house, walled gardens and back lawn' and division 10 is 'the front lawn'. There are fields named 'clover', 'pigeon house', 'quarry', 'brick' and 'bullock' and several 'parks', varying in size between four and seven acres; division 18 was marked as 'bog enclosed to be reclaimed'.[24] (Traditional field names persist for many generations and there is nothing to indicate whether these fields were still used for a dovecote, quarrying or brick making.) Williams's profession as land agent probably explains his liking for maps and another of his commissions survives in a 1763 map of lands at Ballynadrumny, which he leased from Josiah Hort.[25]

Like Williamstown, the contemporary Ballinderry House is a square, three-bay, two-storey rubble-stone house. Nearby Kilglass House is a five-bay, two-storey stone house with a dormer attic and a large Venetian window at the centre of the first floor (fig. 7). It has been tentatively dated to *c*.1725 and its gate lodge and gateway with ornate finials and cast-iron gates are believed to be contemporary.[26] It was presumably the residence at Kilglass Mill, which used to stand nearby.

While the owners of such new houses enjoyed their enhanced surroundings, other members of the community were probably less impressed by their beauty than by what they represented. Solid

7. Kilglass House, an early Georgian residence (by Rachel Clarke)

Georgian farmhouses with good farmyards denoted more efficient farming, agricultural surpluses, more money in the economy and more jobs. While many farms formerly had a random scattering of outbuildings, ordered farmyards increasingly became a feature, often with the house and buildings ranged along two or three sides of a rectangular yard. On estates and larger farms, a formal courtyard was often built, with arched doorways and entrance gate.

An examination of legal transactions of the late seventeenth century and eighteenth century shows that in contrast to the unity and relative stability of the Colley estate, there were complex changes both in landownership and in tenancy in the rest of the barony. The O'Mores were steady landowners at the north-west of the barony and the Palmers, once established, provided stability in the west but the rest of the barony was divided among a number of owners, with many tenants, and there was a sense of flux. There is no doubt that prosperous tenants such as the Medcalfs were eager to become landowners and would take every opportunity in the following century to establish themselves more firmly in the area.

4. The nineteenth century: before and after the Great Famine

The 1798 rebellion caused an unsettled beginning to the nineteenth century across the barony but the continued presence of the More O'Ferralls and the Palmers on their estates had a stabilizing effect. The former seem to have maintained in good order the large estate which they had held since a grant from Elizabeth I in 1574. A fervently religious family, proud of its ancient Irish ancestry, in the eighteenth century its sons were educated at Jesuit colleges in Europe. A long-standing supporter of the clergy, it maintained a private chapel on the estate, where Mass was celebrated until the early twentieth century. Its commitment to the local church and its continued residence in Balyna kept the family closer to its tenants than was the case with the absentee Harbertons or with other non-resident Anglican landlords, who were more distant from their tenants, and more inclined to evict tenants and to be attacked during land agitation later in the nineteenth century.[1]

Major Ambrose More O'Ferrall had served in foreign armies until the death of his father in 1790, when he returned to manage the estate and build a large mansion about 1815. As was common with the Roman Catholic elite, he chose Downside and Stonyhurst for his first three sons' schooling. His daughter Letitia joined the Sisters of Charity and gave money to purchase the house on St Stephen's Green, Dublin, which became St Vincent's Hospital. His eldest son Richard became MP for Kildare in 1830 and held significant government posts until appointed governor of Malta in 1847. He later served two further periods as MP, first for Longford, later for Kildare. After his death in 1880, his son Ambrose inherited Balyna. He stood unsuccessfully for parliament as a Liberal but served as high sheriff of Kildare and Carlow. After Balyna House was accidentally destroyed by fire in 1888, he built the Italianate house which still stands on the land.[2]

The Palmers continued to live on their Rahan estate and their well-ordered workmen's accounts show what was happening on the farm on any given day. For instance, the entry for 31 May 1815 records '3 leading cars, 2 in garden, 1 turning potatoes, 1 at stable, 2 girls weeding oats'. The accounts give an insight into the working year on the farm, enabling one to track the rhythm of the seasons, although an entry for 13 June 1815 for planting potatoes points to a late spring. Numerous entries showing that labourers were working in the garden as opposed to the farm indicate that the Palmers had both the interest and the capacity to devote funds to growing vegetables and fruit and to enhancing their surroundings.[3]

While Lord Harberton was an absentee, conditions on the Colley demesne remained important for the community at the beginning of the nineteenth century. Having been neglected for some years, it was further compromised by the raid in 1798. The second Viscount Harberton let the house and some of the demesne to Lord Tyrawley, who offered to repair it in the hope of securing a lease of the entire demesne. While he conceded that Newberry was 'a very pretty place', he stated that the late Lord Harberton, who had died in April 1798, 'has neglected it, or rather has not laid out one shilling on it for some years past'.[4] Newberry was sold to a later tenant, Edward Wolstenholme, about 1851. Since then it has changed hands three times, most recently in 2010, when it was bought by Wesley Carter, a local beef farmer.

The Colley family, even as absentees, maintained good relations with the tenants, many of whom were of stable Anglican families. Irrespective of religious affiliation, it was in the Colleys' interests to have long-established, peaceable tenants who knew the realities of their situation and felt secure without long leases. One of those tenants was John Holt of Coolavacoose, whose 1801 will illustrates how tenants passed their farms to the next generation in much the same way as landowners did. He made unusual provisions in his will of 1801:

> I leave and bequeath unto my son George Holt all my right title and interest in and to that part of my farm of Coolavacoose which he and my son Thomas Holt are now in possession of; and it is my will that my said son George shall not set said farm

to any other person than his brother Samuel Holt, provided said Samuel will give him 20s. per acre for every acre therein contained yearly during the term he shall set it to him for.[5]

As it turned out, Samuel took over Coolavacoose, which passed to his son John and from father to son in a direct line ever since. The Holt farm journal (1798–1879) makes it clear that the family was well ensconced on the land by then but because that section of Byrn's report is missing, it is unknown at what time they had taken over the tenancy. The journal is neither personal diary nor account book; it mostly records expenditure on labourers but also contains recipes for animal cures and biographical notes relating to the family. The confusing Holt descent continued, alternating John and Samuel in successive generations to Sam Holt (1926–2019), who preserved the journal. The Holts are unusual not because they kept farm journals but because they have retained them for posterity.[6]

One can trace the farming year in the journal, starting with ploughing, harrowing and sowing in winter and spring, cutting and saving hay from May, through reaping in July, August and September, potato digging in October and the lengthy process of threshing. The Holts reared cattle, a few sheep and pigs, and hens, ducks and geese for the table and for eggs. They grew oats and barley, grass for hay and in later years, wheat; they also became breeders of Clydesdale horses. In the early years the farm had two cottages which were rented by the Holts' labourers, while others rented potato ground (sometimes called a potato garden). Many labourers bought oatmeal, potatoes for eating and seed from Holt, all of which reduced the amount they received on settlement. The May 1822 computation for Francis Flanagan showed that his work payment came to £2 15s. 3d. but with his house rent and potato rent and a few other items, he owed £3 9s. 2d. The journal also shows the type of tools used on the farm and the role of local blacksmiths in maintaining them. Such journals rarely offer insights into the personal life of the writer but an 18 November 1857 entry that 'John Holt made a promise to drink no whiskey nor whiskey punch for one year if the Almighty spares me my health' is telling.[7]

The Holts held from year to year and did not have a written lease. While others did have leases, they rarely exceeded thirty-one years or three lives. The *actual* lease to William Clarke of Kishavanna on 13 December 1825 of thirty-five acres of arable land in Clonkeen for life or thirty-one years is a rare survivor in local custody. It comes complete with the parties' and witnesses' signatures and has a well-drawn integrated map of the holding.[8] The Holts and the Clarkes were members of the Church of Ireland, which, although a small minority, played a disproportionate role in society due to its position as the established church and its consequent responsibility to keep public records.

Although each parish was obliged since 1538 to keep a vestry minute book and registers of baptisms, marriages and burials, Carbury vestry records are extant only from 1797 and registers from 1804–5.[9] Much information can be gleaned from the registers. In the first twenty-five years, there were twenty-six marriages, in eighteen of which both bride and groom were Carbury parishioners. The outside partner in six of the other marriages came from a neighbouring parish, such as Edenderry, one came from Queen's Co. (Laois) and one from Dublin. These statistics reveal a localized and stable pattern of settlement in the early years of the nineteenth century but there is not enough information from Roman Catholic parishes to establish whether this held true for the barony as a whole.[10] Of a sample of twenty-six marriages in Derrinturn church between 1870 and 1875, all the brides were from the barony, as were all the grooms, except for two from Dublin and one each from neighbouring Clonbullogue and Robertstown.[11] This information suggests that despite the disruption caused by the Great Famine, the population in the barony continued to be very localized.

Entries in the vestry books are sparse but show how the duty of care to the poor and vulnerable was exercised. This responsibility fell on the Church of Ireland as the established church and while the majority Roman Catholic population resented that tithes were payable to support the Church of Ireland and its clergy, its obligation to support the entire population was onerous.[12] From time to time the vestry minutes show a parish cess was levied to send foundlings to the Foundling Hospital in Dublin. The hospital, which aimed to avoid the death of abandoned children and to raise them within the Church of Ireland, had been operational since 1730 and took in 1,500–2,000 children each year. Such children might be baptized before they left the parish, be entered in the register as a foundling and given a name such as 'Carberry', 'Newberry', 'Field' or 'Spring', to indicate where they had been found. The cost of having a child taken to the hospital was considerable, 11s. 4½d. being paid to an unnamed woman in 1810 for such a task.[13]

Although the main records of the Foundling Hospital are not extant, the whole operation was disastrous. William Wodsworth's exposé in 1876 confirmed its horrors: while some 'foundlings' were indeed found after their abandonment, the governors categorized those who *sent* their children to the Foundling Hospital as the poor, mothers who wished to conceal their disgrace, dissolute parents and those well-off parents who wanted their children to be raised at public expense. This categorization ignored the anguish of a mother who could see no option other than to send a child to the hospital but Wodsworth printed letters from or on behalf of mothers whose child had been taken to the hospital without their consent, often by deception.

The system was rotten even before the child was delivered to the hospital. 'Carrying nurses' often put six or eight infants in a basket in which they transported them. Many of the children suffered from cold and other privations and did not survive the journey. Other infants were left anonymously in the 'cradle' or 'turning gate' at the hospital entrance and were dead or dying when found. Babies who survived were sent out to wet nurses in Dublin, Kildare and Wicklow and if they grew to the age of 7 or 8, they either stayed in the locality or returned to the Foundling Hospital, where their best hope was for an elusive good apprenticeship. Nurses were paid £2 a year to look after a child and had to report with that child to the hospital once a year to secure payment. Most of these women were of the labouring class, for whom such payment was attractive. Some of the children in their care were neglected and abused. Older children sometimes stayed in the area, mostly employed as farm labourers or servants.

The hospital registers made for devastating reading: entries included the admission date, the branding/tattooing of the child for identification, state of health, distance s/he had been brought, details of dispatch to a nurse, elopement, apprenticeship. No greater indictment could be made than the statistics for the twelve years up to June 1796: 25,352 admitted, 11,663 died in the nursery, 5,119 died in the country, 471 died in the family (total: 17,253); 6,442 struck off the books, 1,936 apprenticed, 170 eloped (ran away), 424 given to parents.[14]

Little is known about the parish's handling of the problem of foundlings but an 1815–27 account book lists some who were brought up in Carbury.[15] Each child's name appears with her/his tattoo number and the name of the nurse. It seems appalling that the children were tattooed but it is more understandable when one considers that William Bell was numbered W1481, showing that he was child 1,481 of 1,792 admitted to the hospital in 1820.[16] 'Bell', 'Empson' and 'Sharp' were probably the surnames given in the parish where they had been found and most of the surnames were unfamiliar in Carbury, as the principle prevailed that foundlings should not be sent to the area whence they came. Occasionally, where such children had been born to impoverished families, they *were* sent back but to a different family.

The 'foundling' label was persistent, being inserted in a marriage register where the father's name had to be given. In 1846 both James Cope and Ellen McKenzy were given as foundlings, as was Thomas Spring, who married Matilda Phillips, daughter of a tenant farmer in the parish. The Copes vanish from parish records after the baptism of a son in 1847 and do not appear in subsequent public records.[17] Spring, a labourer, moved from farm to farm at Carrick and Williamstown until he became a land steward at Greenhill, Ballyburly.

One of the principal ways to help people was by education. Considerable strides in primary education were made in the nineteenth century, as can be seen in developments in Carbury. In 1800 it was still officially the responsibility of the Church of Ireland to educate every child but that often did not happen. Charles Lindsay, bishop of Kildare, in reporting on two visitations of the diocese, showed great concern that the church should fulfil its obligations and was broad-minded in his approach. In Kill, for instance, he noted that there was neither church school nor schoolmaster but 'an excellent master of the Roman Catholic persuasion who teaches within half a mile of the church'.[18] In Geashill, he recorded with equanimity that the parish school had sixty pupils, the majority of whom were Roman Catholics.[19] He was anxious that there should be a school in each parish. In Killashee, the parish clerk was 'ready to keep a school' but there was no building. Some months later, Lindsay observed that 'no notice had been taken' to remedy the deficiency, so he ordered that a schoolmaster be provided.[20]

In Carbury, he recorded William Angier as schoolmaster in 1804 and William Richmond in 1808, with a house, two acres and an annual salary of £2, the land having been given by Lord Harberton.[21] That he made no comment about Richmond's running of Carbury school is a positive sign. No indication is given of its size or composition but Richmond's salary, even allowing for a free house, was relatively low. In Mountmellick, the schoolmaster was paid a salary of £15 and 'teaches 15 children and charges for the tuition of other children: average 40'.[22] In Ballykean, where there was no church but a large Anglican population, the schoolmaster's salary was £5.[23] As in Mountmellick, Richmond supplemented his salary by having paying pupils. The Holt children of Coolavacoose attended the parish school in the 1810s and Richmond was paid partly in cash, partly in seed potatoes and pigs and in having his turf drawn for him.[24]

The attention that Lindsay paid to primary education shows that he understood its potential to provide new employment opportunities in a fast-growing population.[25] In 1810, from a population approaching six million, there were only 23,000 children in school.[26] The poor state of Irish education had been exposed by the report of an Irish parliamentary commission appointed in 1788,[27] but no action was taken. Soon after the Act of Union, the Westminster parliament established a new commission, which examined Irish secondary and primary education. It suggested that a permanent board of education should be created, which would establish a national system of education and provide new schools under its control where necessary. The commissioners were adamant that there should be no denominational religious education and that training colleges were needed to provide adequate teachers.[28] Although a board of education was established, its remit ran only to endowed schools and their recommendations on primary education were ignored. It was, however, against this background that the Society for Promoting the Education of the Poor of Ireland was founded in 1811 to provide a 'well-ordered' education to 'all classes of professing Christians without any attempt to interfere with the peculiar religions of any'.[29] Commonly called the Kildare Place Society, it established a teacher-

8. Clonkeen School, opened by the Church Education Society (by Rachel Clarke)

training college and funded the building and operation of schools throughout the country.[30] A decade later, there were twenty-five schools in Co. Kildare under its auspices, including one at Carbury and another at Clonkeen (fig. 8).[31]

The situation noted by Bishop Lindsay, in which Roman Catholic children often attended their local Church of Ireland school, continued but Derrinturn had a Roman Catholic school by 1815 and Carbury had one by 1824. (An application in 1838 by Fr Edward Earle, the parish priest of Derrinturn, for improvements to its school was supported by the Church of Ireland community.)[32] Landlords often encouraged their Roman Catholic tenants to send their children to the local Church of Ireland school. This was not necessarily a proselytizing act, for it may have been motivated by the wish for such children to have an education which would enable them to find employment. The Roman Catholic authorities, however, did not approve and were increasingly vociferous in their demand for a national school system. Catholic emancipation in 1829 strengthened their position in many spheres and their educational aspirations were realized in 1831 by the formation of the National Board for Education to administer a national school system. This was a major turning point, for the board removed financial pressure from local communities by giving grants for building schools and paying teachers' salaries. Not only was the curriculum to be non-denominational in the sense that children of all faiths could attend their local national school; there were to be positive efforts to encourage children of all faiths to learn to live together in tolerance. Religious teaching was to be entirely separate from secular education. While the national school system proved a great benefit to the Roman Catholic community, the prohibition of religious reference within the curriculum did not win acceptance. All the denominations believed that religious education was an integral part of education but the Roman Catholic and Presbyterian churches decided to join the national school scheme and work from within to change its rules on denominational education while the Church of Ireland tried to create its own education system by withdrawing from the scheme and establishing the Church Education Society in 1839. It was well endowed initially and it flourished for some years and largely took over the role of the Kildare Place Society. The Church of Ireland schools in Carbury village and at Clonkeen were transferred to its control and two other schools were established within the parish.[33]

Church Education Society schools were open to children of all faiths (no consideration was given to the possibility of atheism) and although the reading of the Authorized Version of the Bible was prescribed for all, only Church of Ireland children had to learn Anglican doctrine. Roman Catholics were not necessarily put off sending their children to a Church Education Society school. For example, in 1867 there were seven Church of Ireland and thirteen Roman Catholic pupils in Clonkeen school. The most likely reason for the large proportion of Roman Catholics was that Clonkeen was some distance from a school of their own denomination but the royal commissioners on primary education in Ireland, appointed in 1868, were concerned that there might have been an element of compulsion in their attendance and quizzed the local Church Education Society inspector on the subject. Asked why there were so many Roman Catholics, he could give no reason and on being pressed, answered with a *non sequitur*: 'there were always Roman Catholics'. He gave assurances that he had not heard of any pressure to attend.[34]

There was less and less need for Roman Catholics to send their children to Church of Ireland schools as the national education system became established. For most of the eighteenth century, due to the penal laws, Roman Catholics had been reduced to worshipping in mass houses, often small thatched buildings, but as the laws were relaxed, church building began in the 1790s and it accelerated greatly after Catholic emancipation. In the ensuing century, more than 3,000 churches were built in Ireland, funded by parishioners rich and poor, often with contributions from local Anglicans.[35] Across the barony of Carbury a network of Roman Catholic churches and national schools developed. Holy Trinity Church, Derrinturn, built *c.*1809, was the first, followed later in the century by St Patrick's Church, Johnstown Bridge (1830), Holy Family Church, Kilshanroe (*c.*1849, replaced in 1975), St Mary's Church, Broadford (1856), and St Brigid's Church, Clogherinkoe (1862).

The link between parish and school was cemented in the 1870s when the Liberal government of W.E. Gladstone bowed to pressure from the Roman Catholic authorities in allowing a denominational national school system to develop. When he became prime minister in 1868, it was his avowed mission to pacify Ireland and he sought to accomplish it by implementing a fairer settlement across Irish society. By then, the Church of Ireland generally accepted that it could not maintain a separate system and that it would have to join the national education system. The national schools eventually bore fruit but one should treat the literacy figures in the censuses with care. The increase in the proportion of those who were literate from 26 per cent in 1841 to 41.85 per cent in 1861 reflected not so much the improvement in education as the decline in population, for the number who could read and write declined slightly (2,571 to 2,469). The fact remained that many families could not afford to send their children to school and needed them to work on the land.[36]

The condition of children in the barony reflects that of the whole population. The great majority of the working population of Co. Kildare in 1841 was classified as labourers and servants. Small holdings of five acres or less made up 40 per cent of the total acreage.[37] Labourers were often paid with food rather than cash and were heavily dependent on their employer's goodwill. Even if they did receive a wage, it often fluctuated with the seasons and some had no work except at harvest.

The labourers' vulnerability was demonstrated by the 1845 evidence of Richard Grattan to the Devon Commission on land occupation in Ireland. He considered himself a good landlord but stated that:

If I were to pay them money, I could not employ one half of them. I pay them with the produce of the land instead of paying them in money and obliging them to go to Edenderry – five miles there five miles back; I pay them with potatoes and accommodate them so far as the saving of time is concerned. The labourer is accommodated as well as myself, because he saves us time and labour, and I am not obliged to send my horses and carts to market. I get oatmeal ground for them and I pay the balance in money. Many farmers do the same.[38]

In 1816 James Brownrigg, Lord Downshire's agent, had reported widespread distress among the labouring classes, who were 'nearly starving in the midst of plenty' and were in consequence 'beginning to grow turbulent'.[39] Even before the Great Famine, many labourers were unemployed and, in a crisis, they were the first to need help. In 1838 the entire country was divided into poor-law unions, one of which was the Edenderry Poor-Law Union, with a remit extending to Carbury and the surrounding townlands. The building of a workhouse began and it opened just in time, as it was quickly filled by famine victims. Designed for 600 inmates, it was soon full to overflowing and may have had as many as 1,800 at the worst of the Great Famine.[40] Workhouses, along with dispensaries, county infirmaries, fever hospitals, courts and jails, were part of a system that emerged in the nineteenth century, financed through a land tax called county cess rather than by tithes.[41] Before the introduction of social welfare in the twentieth century, there was very little protection for the weakest members of society and many died in destitution. It is difficult to know whether the 'two idiot men' who were voted financial support from Carbury church collections in 1882 fared better than those who were sent to the lunatic asylum or the workhouse.[42]

As in the previous century, the Colley estate had been divided between Lord Harberton and his brother, who took the name George F. Colley. In the spring of 1846, in the face of a second year of famine, they applied for funding to buy enough corn for 'a joint estate of about 6,000 acres, inhabited by an exclusively rural population of about 2,500 souls of all classes',[43] and the agent was told to provide employment for all. Famine works included the digging of field drains and laying of stone shores on tenant farms, an initiative which proved useful to succeeding generations. A poor-relief committee was set up in January 1847. It was chaired by Edward Wolstenholme, the tenant at Newberry, who was already chairman of the Edenderry Board of Guardians. The joint secretaries were the Church of Ireland vicar, the Revd Francis Hewson, and Fr James Phelan of Carbury and Dunfierth, while Fr James Murphy of Derrinturn was treasurer. As famine worsened during that year, the committee distributed cornmeal free or at reduced rates to the poor, while putting pressure on the government to give aid. Local landowners, of whom 75 per cent were members of the Church of Ireland, contributed generously to the relief fund but the harsh winter led to more families being dependent.[44]

Richard Grattan had a disastrous reaction when he tried to help his tenants by buying corn for them. When his servants refused to eat it, he said his own family would have it for breakfast, after which they all were ill and his 15-year-old son Richard died. Two servants accused of poisoning him were acquitted on the basis that they had wanted to injure but not kill the family.[45] Grattan did not abandon his efforts on behalf of the poor and his obituary recorded that he 'died far from affluent on account of having financially exhausted himself in endeavouring to relieve the starving people in his locality in the dark days of 1847'.[46]

The Carbury area, principally the labouring classes, would have suffered more severely in the Great Famine had the cattle and sheep farmers not played such a significant role in the local economy. As they had a smaller proportion of their land in tillage, less labour was needed for the harvest and consequently there were fewer vulnerable labourers than in a barony where tillage predominated. Potatoes *were* grown locally and were an important part of the diet but the fact that they did not dominate the economy saved the area from worse suffering. This is clear from the statistics for the percentage of the Irish population which claimed rations in the summer of 1847: less than 30 per cent in the Carbury area, compared with more than 60 per cent in much of the west.[47]

While the decline in Kildare's population was sharpest between 1841 and 1851, it was continuous from 1831 to 1901. The census figures reflect not only excess deaths during the Famine but the emigration and displacement of agricultural labourers and their families, who were its principal victims. In 1831 there were almost 1,700 families employed in agriculture across the barony of Carbury; by 1841 that number had fallen to 1,150 and there were only 494 families thus employed in 1861. A partial explanation of what was happening before the Famine was given by Grattan in 1845, when he stated that in Carbury

> proprietors are endeavouring to consolidate the farms until they reach 100 to 150 Irish acres so as to cause them to be occupied by a different class of person ... This movement presses heavily upon the labourers and small class of farmer. In some cases, the landlords give money to pay for the passage of the former occupiers to Canada or the United States.[48]

(In speaking of Irish acres, Grattan ignored the widespread adoption of statute acres, under which 100 acres became 162 statute acres.)

While the Famine was caused by dependence on the potato and the outbreak of blight, the situation for the labouring poor was made much worse by the attitude of the government. It was dismissive of the Irish and saw the opportunities afforded by the Famine for agrarian modernization and the clearance of agricultural labourers. This view was to some extent shared by landowners, and those who made no notable efforts towards famine relief lost the respect in which they had been held in the community.

The displacement of the labourers is directly reflected in the census figures for the number of houses in the barony. The way in which houses were classified was rather crude, relying on the number of rooms and windows and the durability of the building materials. Fourth-class houses had only one room and one window and were built of cob or some other perishable material; third-class houses were better, having up to four rooms and as many windows, while a good farmhouse with five to nine rooms and windows was placed in the second class and anything more elaborate was a first-class house. In the twenty years from 1841 to 1861, first-class houses showed a small increase and second-class houses increased from 168 to 204 but there was a huge decline in third-class houses, from 1,115 to 660 and fourth-class houses halved in number from 344 to 173. In the landscape, this would initially have manifested itself in an increased number of uninhabited poor houses but those which had been built with cob and thatch soon disappeared into the ground.

The population of Carbury village fell from 128 people in 21 houses in 1841 to 96 people in 20 houses in 1851 and continued to fall for the rest of the century. There *were* gains, however: by 1871 there was a post office and Dr William Waters was the resident surgeon in the dispensary.[49] In the 1870s, a branch of the Midland and Great Western Railway was built between Enfield and Edenderry, with a station at Carbury. From 1881 the presence of the railway enabled a well-attended annual sports day in the village but it declined within a few years because the railway company refused to run an evening return train to Enfield. More significantly, the station enabled cattle to be taken to Dublin for sale and proved a boon to local farmers.

The Famine increased the indebtedness of many Irish landlords who had long lived beyond their means. While there might have been a specific reason for getting into debt, such as the costs of building a great house or standing for parliament, even these considerations were not as significant as the extravagance and poor business management of many landlords and the often-recurring obligation to provide for widows and younger children on the death of an owner and consequent succession of his eldest son. While in some counties efforts at famine relief increased a landlord's indebtedness to the point where he had to sell large tracts of land under the Encumbered Estates Act of 1849, the Carbury area was not greatly affected due to the dominance of the Colley, More O'Ferrall and Palmer estates. Nevertheless, there were landowners whose long-term debt became unsustainable under the extra pressure of the Famine, while the creditors, who had never experienced serious difficulty in foreclosing on mortgage arrears, were enabled by the 1849 act to petition for a sale when encumbrances were more than 50 per cent of an estate's net rent. One of the most prominent landowners to lose land in Kildare in this way was the earl of Milltown, much of whose land in Kildare and other counties came under the remit of the encumbered estates court.

Within the farming community, recovery after the Famine was remarkably quick. Agricultural prosperity from the early 1850s to the late 1870s was largely based on store cattle, butter and sheep and with the growing local emphasis on pasture rather than tillage, farmers

9. Coonagh House, modelled on Newberry Hall (by Rachel Clarke)

sought to increase their holdings further. This development was reflected in Griffith's valuation, a nationwide valuation of property to determine liability to pay the poor rate in each poor-law union, published for Kildare in 1854. It gave detailed information on where people lived and how much property they owned or rented (in statute acres), revealing that the barony of Carbury had a greater proportion of large farmers with a minimum total valuation of £100 than any other part of west Kildare. The valuation was a highly organized process, starting with a list of townlands supplied by the local grand jury and using scientific topographical techniques to mark the boundaries. In the case of a disputed boundary, a meresman would walk the land. Even a systematic survey such as this includes mistakes, as in listing John 'Mathers', correctly Mather, as tenant at Teelough of 'Lord Carbery', correctly Lord Harberton. The valuation shows some changes in townland names since Byrn's 1744 report, such as Clonmeen, being listed as Ballygibbon East and West and part of Oldcourt as Coolavacoose.

On the Colley estate, some of the 1744 farms had been broken up, the largest of these being the 811 acres that the Grattans formerly held at Clonmeen and Rinahan. While the latter remained undivided and was held by Denis Duggan, the former had been divided into several farms, in which Duggan, Daniel and William Jackson, Henry and

Thomas Mather, Thomas Sale, John Smith and James Walsh each had more than 100 acres.

The valuation showed that of the 1744 tenant families only four were definitely still on the same land. At Coonagh, James Boylan had increased the 85-acre holding of which his ancestor was under-tenant to more than 200 acres (fig. 9). He lived there and leased out six houses, each with a small amount of land. In Clonkeen, the Coffeys and du Boes were the only remaining families, the Diggens and the Dowdalls having been replaced by a proliferation of tenants, many with no more than a house and garden.[50] The valuation map shows small houses dotted along the road to Kishavanna, where none of the 1744 tenants remained and they had similarly been replaced by a large number of tenants, most of whom had very little land.[51] The Sales were the most stable and successful of the 1744 tenants. At that time, Samuel Sale held land in Coolgreany, Longridge and Coolcor, where his entire holding won Byrn's approval. In 1854 Samuel Sale retained the 170 acres in Coolcor and had an additional 33 acres in Clonkeen and 44 acres in Carbury, while Thomas Sale held 90 acres at Ardkill and 100 acres in Ballygibbon East.

The Grattans, Paynes and Hursts were still in the barony but on different land and it is likely that Denis Duggan was of the same family as Francis Duggan in Freagh in 1744. Richard and James McCann, who had lands in three townlands, were perhaps descendants of Patrick McCann, undertenant at Collinstown in 1744. That none of the other 1744 families still occupied land in the barony in 1854 shows that there had been a large turnover of tenants in a little over a century, although some of the same families were perhaps, through marriage, *in situ* under a different name. Where a tenancy was in the hands of 'partners' in 1744, there is a sense that theirs was an investment rather than a commitment to farm the land and it is not surprising that the Flinns do not feature among the 1854 tenants of Collinstown, formerly held by Christopher Flinn and partners. Of the townlands whose tenancies had completely changed since 1744, John Payne's former large farm at Ardkill had been divided in three: in addition to Sale's 90 acres, William Murphy and James Flanagan both had farms of more than 200 acres.

While townlands such as Clonkeen and Kishavanna had become fragmented, the opposite happened at Haggard. None of the 1744 tenant families was still there in 1854, at which time most of it was held by Samuel Holt. He had prospered and in 1842 built a new house on his land to replace the one he formerly occupied. An ambitious cousin of the Holts at Coolavacoose, he had married Ann Grattan, sister of Dr John Grattan. Samuel's son Samuel made a good marriage to Anna Maria Jellett and they reared their large family at Carbury House. This branch of the Holts moved in higher social circles than their cousins at Coolavacoose, to the extent that they attended state receptions in Dublin Castle.[52]

The fullest picture of a middle-sized farm in Carbury in the years before and after the Famine is given in John C. Duggan's history of the Duggan family of Highfield. He prints the deeds relevant to their farm, showing that in 1803 Andrew Mullowney obtained a lease of 100 Irish acres at Highfield from the Colley estate. It contained restrictions that he was, on pain of a fine of 10s. a barrel, to give any malt, corn or grist used by him to be ground at Kilmore mill and that in the last two years of the lease, he would not dispose of any 'muck' or compost which was made on the premises. He was also to plant within three years at least two roods of young trees, surrounded by ditches at least six feet wide and five feet deep. These were to be of whitethorn and ash and a hefty penalty of £20 per annum would be incurred if he failed to comply.[53] Mullowney's interest in the lease passed on his death in 1808 to his son-in-law, Patrick Duggan. Patrick and his family lived at Highfield in a thatched cottage until he made over the farm to his son Denis in 1838, at which time the latter was building a new Georgian-style house on the land for his future wife, Maria Hill of Grange. Denis was a successful farmer, who kept his accounts with care and had a ledger in which he entered births, deaths, marriages and departures for school of his large family. It was probably due to his example that the family retained these and the relevant legal papers for posterity.

The accounts reveal that the farm was not much affected during the Famine and that he continued to sell potatoes to his employees, even in the years of the worst blight. One must assume that he was not growing the dreaded Lumper potato, the most vulnerable to blight. The accounts give the wages at different times and show that, like the Holts and Boylans, he often paid in kind and advanced money for clothes, shoes and items such as tobacco. A stock list from May 1855 indicates that the five labourers and three women servants on his 165-acre farm would have been fully employed in providing for his family, his sheep, cattle, pigs and horses.[54] The list reveals that he was a major sheep farmer as the flock exceeded 300 (99 ewes, valued at £2 each on average), 96 hoggets (£1 10s.), 106 lambs (£1) and one ram (£7). As to cattle, he had 14 milk cows (£15 each), 12 'dry fattening' (£11), 10 two-year-old bullocks (£8), 15 two-year-old heifers (£8), 7 yearling heifers (£6), 5 yearling bullocks (£5), 1 yearling bull (£7), a seven-year-old bull (£10) and 13 calves (£2 10s.), constituting a considerable herd. The value of the stock was given as an impressive £1,312 and it had increased by nearly 50 per cent in 1856, indicating the speed of agricultural recovery. The thirteen divisions of the farm are listed, with each field name. The origins of 'mill field' and 'hazelditch field' are obvious but others, such as 'Carey's croft' and 'near combshop' might repay research along with field names on other farms in the barony.

The Duggans did not have long leases but like other Colley tenants of the time were so assured of their future that they built a sizeable house. According to Homan Potterton, the Sales of Ardkill were only tenants from year to year when they built a substantial new house in 1820.[55] Their demonstration of confidence in their security was justified, for they held the farm until they were able to buy it under the land acts. Ardkill provides an example of landholdings changing through marriage: Martha, daughter of Thomas and Alice (née Holt) Sale, married Richard William Potterton of Rathcormick, Co. Meath, in 1853. As she had no brothers, she and her husband inherited Ardkill and passed it to their elder son Thomas. One of Thomas's brothers, Richard William Potterton II, bought Posseckstown, Enfield, while one of his sons, Thomas Edward, inherited Rathcormick and moved to Co. Meath. Thomas's line of Pottertons has remained at Ardkill and subsequent generations have spread to new locations around Carbury. It is striking that a love of sheep has persisted in the family, as can be seen in the Potterton family's continued status as breeders and in Godfrey's role as chair of the North Kildare IFA Sheep Producer Group and as a judge.

Although they were quite conservative and plain Georgian-style houses, Ardkill, Haggard and Highfield demonstrate the nineteenth-century trend towards bigger and more impressive houses. At

Drummin, the Grattans enlarged the house, altering it so that the front door faced the drive, but the most notable building exploits were Balyna House (already noted) and Ballindoolin House, with handsome stable yard and gate lodge, which Humphrey Bor built in 1822; both houses built not by tenants but by landowners, who were more inclined to be ambitious in their building schemes. While such houses demonstrated optimism for the future of farming, over the next century it was largely the strong tenant farmers who prevailed. Much change in landholding has occurred but the Berminghams, Clarkes, Dempseys, Duggans, Holts, Sales/Pottertons and Tyrrells are among the families listed in 1854 who farm the same land today.

5. The nineteenth century: land reform

By the late 1860s, more than two-thirds of land in the barony was given over to grazing and a large proportion of the remaining land produced hay for winter feeding. It was obvious that, while the number of farm labourers had declined greatly since the Famine and the landlords had suffered to a varying extent, the strong tenant farmers benefited in being freed of the cottier class, enjoying many good years as cattle and sheep farmers. They were, moreover, more independent-spirited than before and, emboldened by the lassitude or weakness of most of the landlords, began to aspire to owning their land. The profitability of the farms led to the landlords increasing the rents whenever a lease came up for renewal and these increases were a further spur to the demand for ownership.

While the landlords raised rents, both they and the tenant farmers gradually had to raise the wages of their farm labourers. In trying to estimate the average wage in the years before and after the Great Famine, one must take account of multiple factors. The few surviving farm accounts show that rates of pay varied according to the age and experience of the workers, whether they were paid by the day or at a yearly rate and whether they had a house on the farmer's land. For instance, in July 1830 Samuel Holt of Coolavacoose hired Laurence Casey at 5*d*. per day and Laurence Martin at £5 per year and in 1832 he hired Thomas Martin at £2 per year. In addition, specific tasks were paid at a higher rate, with 1*s*. 4*d*. to 1*s*. 7*d*. per day for mowing, down through reaping, threshing and potato digging at 8*d*. to 1*s*. 6*d*., while lesser jobs such as drawing hay were paid at about 6*d*. per day. The Holts paid less than some farmers but gave their workers a considerable bonus by providing meals.

The difficulty in calculating the average wage is increased by the many concessions made. For instance, in May 1869 Michael Langan was hired on the Boylans' farm at Coonagh at 6*d*. per day: 'he to have his house and garden for £1 10s. per annum, with the grass for one cow and £1 15s. to buy hay'. On the same day, John Farrell was hired 'to act as herd and preserve the stock from bog, dog and thief. He is also to have his house and garden, grass of two cows and £1 15s. to buy hay for one of them, he is to get two lambs in the yeaning season, grass for them till November'. Deductions were also made for money given to employees to buy clothes, shoes and stockings, to give to the priest or to their parents. Lizzie Tyrrell was hired on the Holts' farm in April 1876 for £1 per quarter. By the end of the year, she had received 9s. for boots and 2s. 6d. for soles, 1s. 8d. for a jacket, 1s. each for stockings and ribbon and 2s. for calico. The following spring, she received 1s. 6d. to go to the races and the relatively large sum of 7s. to buy a brooch.[1]

Increased prosperity encouraged farmers to experiment with different crops. For instance, in 1869 Robert Stronge of Clonkeen sought advice on growing kohlrabi, stating that he planned to plant three-and-a-half acres after winter vetches.[2] Later that year, he instructed Edenderry auctioneer Joseph Dowdall to sell at Clonkeen three milch cows, thirteen 2½-year-old heifers and bullocks, forty-six each of hogget ewes and wethers, ten horses, seven haggard stacks of Black Tartary oats, two haggard cocks or pikes of prime upland hay, three acres of swede turnips, 1½ acres each of kohlrabi and rape, 'prime feeding', and one acre of mangel wurtzel. He was also to sell 'seven large haggard stacks Chevalier barley; six large haggard stacks Black Tartary oats; and five acres of rape and turnips' at Coolagh, near Robertstown.[3] This gives useful information, as there are few indications of the varieties of oats and barley grown in Carbury at that time. Whether for equine or human consumption, oats were all types of common oat (*Avena sativa*), of which Black Tartary became popular in the later nineteenth century for animal feed. Chevalier barley was developed in England in the 1820s and its superior qualities made it a world-leading malting barley. No specific mention of the grass seed mixtures used in Carbury has been found but seed merchants' lists suggest that they were native grasses, such as Cocksfoot, Meadow Foxtail and Timothy, with perennial and rye grass and white and red clover.

By 1870 land reform had become a central demand and the British prime minister, W.E. Gladstone, introduced the first of several land acts which addressed tenant/landlord relations. Its modest aims were to provide tenant security and compensation for improvements made but it marked the beginning of the progression to tenant ownership by allowing tenants to buy their holdings if the landlord was willing to sell.[4] The complexity of the provisions of the 1870 Land Act for compensation for improvements led to much litigation. Samuel Holt of Carbury House made a claim to register the improvements which he and his late father, also Samuel, had made at Haggard in building a new house and offices (audaciously estimated at £4,379), herd's house, gates and piers, draining and reclaiming of bog, replacing old fences and planting new ones with quicks (for new hedges), twelve field gullets across new ditches and '15 cabins thrown down and their appurtenances turned into pasture', the entire claim being for £8,166.[5] Samuel's claim was one of the first to be made and was therefore widely reported. Irrespective of the assessment of his case, the details of his works on the land are interesting for what they reveal about contemporary improvements. The stereotypical view is of the landlord evicting tenants. In this case, Samuel Holt, himself a tenant, had a casual disregard for those whom he had evicted, although it is quite conceivable that the cabins had already been abandoned.

Claims were decided by the chairman of the civil-bill courts, appeals being taken to the assizes and then to the court which had been newly established for land cases. Some 2,222 cases were resolved in the courts in the years 1871–7, resulting in 1,420 compensation awards and 802 dismissals.[6] Holt's claim was comprehensively considered and many aspects were accepted but his central claim on the new house was dismissed on the basis that compensation had effectively been given when, in 1844, Harberton 'was so pleased with the house that at Mr Holt's request, he gave him a second farm' and granted a new lease of both farms at a low rent. Some of the newspaper reports alluded to Harberton's generous dealings with Holt on the farm.

Local lore has always held that Samuel gave up his farm and emigrated after a row with Harberton over shooting rabbits on the estate but the cause must have been the blow to his pride due to his lost case. He still had a good house and farm at Haggard, his home at Carbury House and additional land but in 1873 he emigrated with his family to America, where he established himself as a farmer in Kansas. Unsurprisingly, his family flourished there.[7] He sold his interest in Haggard to Frederick Pilkington of Newberry Hall for a hefty £7,000 and gradually disposed of his other Irish assets.[8] This unusual case of emigration removed one of the parish's most forceful characters. Haggard is unusual in Carbury in that it has regularly changed hands by sale rather than by inheritance.

The 1871 list of Irish landowners gives 'owners' of more than one acre, their acreage and valuation, including those with the right of perpetual renewal but that number also includes tenants with leases longer than ninety-nine years.[9] It reveals a contrast between the east of the county, where large tracts of land were owned by the duke of Leinster and a small number of Anglo-Irish, and the barony of Carbury, where the only estates exceeding 2,000 acres were those of the Colleys, More O'Ferralls and Palmers. Few of the large owners could trace their ancestors on the land as far back as the Civil Survey, two centuries earlier. It is easy to miss a Carbury landowner on the list, as the address given is that of his/her residence rather than of the landholding, which is not named. Approximately half of those who owned estates of 500 acres and more were not resident in the county, so much of the land was in the hands of tenants, who were working farmers.

By 1871 'owners' of farms of more than 500 acres included William Loftus Bor, Richard Grattan, Frederick Pilkington, John Gaffney of Ballybrack, Mary Hemmingway of Ballinakill Lower and George Nicolls of Garrisker, while others, including Francis and George Metcalf of Johnstown, had increased the size of their farms to a lesser extent. This was achieved in various ways, such as inheritance, family settlements and mortgages, the purchase of land under the Encumbered Estates Act of 1849 and reclaiming bogland.[10] After the tentative first Irish land act in 1870, successive land acts made it increasingly easy for tenants of the large estates in Carbury to buy their farms but even before that some farmers began effectively to buy their land, as the case of Henry Mather of Brookville shows. In 1854 he was one of the most powerful tenant farmers in Carbury, occupying more than 1,200 acres, which had a combined rateable value exceeding £900. Although he was still taking new short leases from Harberton twenty years later, in 1857 he obtained from Harberton a fee-farm grant of 299 acres, some of which he had previously held as tenant from year to year.[11] (The fee-farm grant gave a perpetual lease and gave him the status of a freeholder.) Mather lived long to enjoy the fruits of his work, dying in 1882 at the age of 93, an exemplar for the ambitious tenant who wanted to buy his land.

Although the government had begun to address the inequity of landholding in the 1870 act, years of bad harvests brought the threat of famine in the late 1870s and the drive for tenant ownership accelerated. The Irish National Land League was founded in 1879 to achieve the three Fs (fair rent, fixity of tenure and free sale) and ultimately to bring about tenant ownership of land. Amidst much local agitation, an attempted landlord's sale of tenants' cattle at Carbury in May 1881 was long recalled by local people. In something of a test case, William and Arthur Murphy, James Boylan and Arthur Smith had asked their landlord, Henry F. Colley, for a reduction in rent to the level of Griffith's valuation and, on refusal, had requested a 20 per cent reduction. Colley again refused and took legal action to recover the rent, in default of which he sought the sale of cattle. It attracted several thousand people, young and old, who converged on the village, dressed in holiday attire. They stood around enjoying the music provided by three bands. The fun of the fair was further suggested by the presence of a goat and a donkey wearing tenant-right placards but a heavy military/police guard was there to control a threatening situation. Amid loud banter and sham bidding, one of Boylan's animals was sold and he then agreed to pay the rent. This proved a precedent, whereby one animal was sold from each lot of his remaining cattle and those of the other three farmers and most of the cattle returned to the fields.[12]

Serious threats of violence arose after land agent Garrett Tyrrell of Ballinderry evicted a tenant from the Armit estate at Castlejordan in the summer of 1881. This led to a huge demonstration and the fact that one of the leading speakers was a local curate, Fr John Wyer, made the situation divisive. As threats of violence increased, some landowners carried guns for their personal safety and Garrett Tyrrell and his brother William J.H. Tyrrell needed armed guards at their houses.[13] The latter was also unpopular for his conduct as a land agent and JP for Kildare and had suffered agrarian violence on his estate for some years. He and Garrett 'were regularly denounced from Land League platforms. It was during this time that William J.H. Tyrrell earned the soubriquet of "Billy the Devil" from local nationalists'.[14]

The 1881 Land Act provided tenant rights to fair rent, fixity of tenure and freedom of sale, and established the Irish Land Commission and Land Court, to which tenants could apply for a judicial rent to be fixed for fifteen years. Neither the 1870 nor the 1881 act went far enough to entice the average tenant to attempt to buy his land and relatively few did so before the 1885 Land Act, whose provisions were more generous. With forty-nine years to repay the government loan at a reduced 4 per cent interest, the response was almost instant and more than 25,000 Irish tenants purchased their land in the three years up to 1888. Presumably all the tenants received the same letter as Patrick Duggan did from Harberton's agent, offering to sell him the fee and pay all costs involved in the sale, giving him a fortnight to reply and stipulating that no sale would take place unless a quorum of tenants agreed to buy.[15] That the Colleys facilitated the process is demonstrated in the Registry of Deeds by rafts of sales on the same day, as on 14 February 1888, when William Jackson of Ballygibbon West, Thomas and William Sale jointly and William R. Smith, all of Ballygibbon East bought 115, 106 and 120 acres respectively.[16]

The effect of this and further land acts was such that in 1895, when William Clarke began his accounts as agent for the Colley estate, there was only a small number of tenants left. The process was largely completed after the Wyndham Land Act of 1903, which, with an element of compulsion, encouraged landlords to sell their entire estate. On average, they received the equivalent of twenty-two years' rent, with a bonus of 12 per cent if they sold their entire estate. Tenants were given until the 1970s to complete the purchase of their land by paying an annuity to the Irish Land Commission. These annuities were considerably less than their previous rents, so the vast majority of tenants availed of the act in the next few years.[17] Thus was effected the greatest social and economic revolution in modern Ireland.

While the Land League achieved many of its aims in the 1881 Land Act, the movement became more radical and the emphasis soon changed from land issues to Home Rule. Church of Ireland fears that the National League might prove sectarian were addressed by Fr Joseph McCrea, the local curate, and secretary of the Carbury branch, who recorded that the membership included 'Protestants who had read the history of Ireland aright and were above such narrow-minded prejudices'.[18] Tenants, irrespective of their religious persuasion, appreciated the rent reductions secured by the league on local estates and while Harberton volunteered a 20 per cent reduction on his estate, the branch secured reductions throughout the district with few evictions. Henry Mather of Ballygibbon was clearly making a point when he was evicted in 1889 from a small part of his holding (sixty acres) on which he was four years in arrears. The secretary of the Carbury branch of the National League, Hugh Bennett, was evicted on the same day but the *Kildare Observer* report added: 'Lord Harberton is one of the best landlords in the country. He has had no evictions on his property this hundred years'.[19] The *Leinster Leader* made the salient comment that 'Mr Mather is a Protestant having strong National sympathies'.[20] A small number of parishioners like him and William Smith of Ballyhagan supported Home Rule but they were a minority within the Church of Ireland. Hostility gradually decreased until a nationalist revival at the time of the 1798 centenary, when there was a large demonstration on Carbury Hill. Agrarian tensions were reduced by the redistribution of land following the Wyndham Land Act.

The growing prosperity of the farming community in the 1860s and 1870s and the increasing of tenant ownership offered better potential for farmers' sons but not all of them chose to stay in Carbury. While, at the height of the Great Famine, emigration was the recourse of the desperate, in the second half of the nineteenth century, it became an increasingly attractive option for the adventurous and ambitious. Apart from Scotland or England, the United States, Canada and Australia were the most frequent destinations but some emigrants went to New Zealand or South Africa. While some struggled, the majority of emigrants from the Carbury area did well. Coming from a farming background, many made a good living but it was those who went into finance, construction and business who became wealthy. Some emigrants made enough money abroad to return and buy land. Occasionally, an emigrant who prospered left money to family members at home with which they might buy land.[21]

Among those who prospered abroad was Richard Clarke, the fourth of nine children of Richard and Ellen Clarke of Clonkeen. While his brothers, William, Thomas and John stayed in the local area, his brother Henry emigrated to Canada and Richard to the

United States in 1888 at the age of 18. He settled in Wallingford, Connecticut, where he was deeply involved in local administration, serving as warden (mayor) of the borough in 1921. A successful career culminated in his co-foundation of a firm of general contractors. With a stated principle that they would 'build into every structure ... permanence of stability, the best of workmanship, with full regard for beauty of architectural design', the business was very successful and completed important churches, schools, hospitals, libraries and banks.[22]

There were, however, still cases of people emigrating in desperation. Among the local families so affected was Charles Payne of Clonkeen House, who seemed to be a successful farmer in the 1850s and 1860s. He had about 200 acres with a good house and a lawn fine enough to stage cricket matches for Carbury Cricket Club. By 1876, however, it seems that he had overreached himself, for he was bankrupt. Clonkeen House and farm and the life-insurance policies for him and his son Charles were sold at auction. According to the *Freeman's Journal* of 5 January 1895, Charles Payne of Clonkeen (presumably the son) left for Australia 'about eighteen years ago' and was last known to be in Sydney. While his father was regarded as a gentleman in the 1860s, Charles was referred to as a labourer on his arrival in Australia in 1877.

While land reform was a vital aspect of Gladstone's mission in Ireland, another was the disestablishment of the Church of Ireland. The Irish Church Act of 1869 ended the system whereby the law of the church (on such matters as marriage) was the law of the land and all were obliged to support the church through tithes. Although the church suffered a considerable loss of income and status at disestablishment, it gained freedom from government control and the new system of church governance was remarkably democratic, with an emphasis on service rather than power. In a time when politics were far from democratic, it was effective in encouraging those from 'the big house' to work as equals with all the other men of the parish for the common good, and the Palmers of Rahan were exemplars. The involvement of the gentry continued but in a place like Carbury they were outnumbered by working farmers, who proved the backbone of parish life. It was a major commitment by one of the latter to become churchwarden, as the duties were demanding. Many

10. Ballindoolin House, built by Humphrey Bor in 1822 (by Rachel Clarke)

were brought up in a tradition of service to church and community and gave freely of their time, as they did in the next century in agricultural organizations.

In the late nineteenth century, the decline of 'the big house' was already discernible. In addition to the sale of Newberry, Ballindoolin (fig. 10) effectively changed hands in the 1890s due to the Bors' financial difficulties. Edward and Charlotte Bor of Ballindoolin had a large family but he died in 1870 at the age of 54 and five of their sons died young. It is difficult for a family to recover from such overwhelming loss and although the eldest surviving son inherited, the Bors could no longer cope financially and left Ballindoolin in the hands of their land agent, William J.H. Tyrrell. Appointed as receiver under a High Court order of 1893, he assumed the management of the estate on behalf of the Bor family. His subsequent proposal to take the tenancy of Ballindoolin House was accepted and he held it until his death in 1933 at the age of 80.

6. The twentieth century: organization and growth

The government hoped that the Wyndham Land Act would end land agitation and reduce the impetus of nationalism. A third attempt to introduce Home Rule was begun in 1912. As progress towards the passing of the legislation in parliament was slowed by Irish Unionist opposition, which included an armed organization called the Ulster Volunteers, the Irish Parliamentary Party formed a paramilitary group called the Irish Volunteers in November 1913. It was to be ready to mobilize to protect the nationalist cause. A branch of the Irish Volunteers was formed in Edenderry in April 1914. A Carbury branch was formed at a meeting after Mass in Derrinturn in July 1914 and 'numerous enrolments were made'.[1] Within a few months, the outbreak of the First World War led the Nationalist leader John Redmond to call on the members of the Irish Volunteers to participate in the war.

While men from the area had volunteered in the early years of the First World War, the threat of conscription in 1918 was so badly received that a greater number joined the IRA. The changing attitude to the war was obvious by the summer of 1916, when a recruiting meeting was held at Carbury. It was attended by 'almost all the public representatives of the district' and addressed by a range of speakers. Charles Colley Palmer, in the chair, showing awareness of the local situation, stated that

> they were there ... to ask [the men] for their own sake, for their country's sake and the sake of their women and children to come forward and fight. They were not asking them to fight for England at all. That was the biggest mistake they could make. Ireland has never been in greater peril than it [is] in now.[2]

Only two men enlisted after the meeting.

There had been no rush of farmers to volunteer as, although they were now landowners, most did not have enough education to become officers yet considered themselves superior to the rank and file. Another consideration was the need to produce food and the profitability of farming during the war, as the value of agricultural produce doubled. About 100 enlisted, of whom thirty-two died.[3] The only death which affected the succession on a large farm was that of William Mather, son of Edward Mather and Ada Bor of Brookville, who died at the Somme on 13 October 1916. His daughter, Willa Mather, died at Brookville in 2007 in the bed in which she was born ninety years earlier, shortly after his death.[4] Her mother remained a widow, Willa did not marry and the farm was sold when she died. Of those who survived the war, William J.H. Tyrrell's son, William Upton Tyrrell, was one of the first to enlist. His father, believing that, as a prominent public figure, he had to be seen to support the war effort, sent the local newspapers regular updates from his son's letters. It is likely that his missives served only to remind locals of how much they disliked him. Although Willie survived the war, like so many servicemen, he was physically and emotionally damaged and never returned to Carbury.

Local people were fearful about civil strife after the 1916 Rising and members of the Church of Ireland became anxious when the Tyrrells of Ballindoolin received copies of oaths, allegedly found on prisoners in Dublin, committing 'Sinn Féiners' to massacring all Protestants.[5] Tyrrell was vulnerable as he was a vocal Unionist and had previously organized local meetings to oppose Home Rule. Once the War of Independence began, he was informed of frequent plans to assassinate him while he performed his duties as land agent and justice of the peace, and his family lived in constant fear. On 28 July 1920 Ballindoolin was attacked by forty-five armed men, who shattered windows and smashed the front door but did not get into the house. Tyrrell shot and wounded two of the raiders but raids continued. In the summer of 1921 the local IRA forwarded to GHQ a list of people, including local justices of the peace and postmasters/mistresses, who were considered a potential threat.[6] On 11 July 1921 raiders tried to burn Ballindoolin, causing much damage, but the calling of the truce that very day may have saved others on the list from harm.

While many, particularly those of the small Church of Ireland community, were nervous, as Terence Dooley points out, during the War of Independence no big house was burned in Kildare, making it one of only six counties in which this was the case. Remarking that 'the extent to which civilians were targeted by the IRA in Kildare never reached the level that it did in more active counties', he contrasts Kildare with Cork, where 146 'spies' or 'informers' were murdered between January 1920 and 11 July 1921, of whom 36 per cent were Protestants and 29 per cent were ex-servicemen, whereas in Kildare, one of the counties with the highest percentages of ex-servicemen, only one was murdered.[7] The granting of independence brought little relief, followed as it was by the Civil War. On 15 December 1922 William Tyrrell was attacked and badly beaten on a farm for which he was agent, his life perhaps saved by the fact that his young son Bobby was with him. It is notable that no houses in the barony were burned during this time and no families fled their farm. This is in contrast to the neighbouring county of Westmeath, where many estates were abandoned and ex-servicemen and members of the RIC left.[8]

While there is no evidence of a major exodus from the barony, the population decline was probably greater than the 8 per cent decrease between 1901 and 1911. If the two censuses are taken together, about 40 per cent of the population was born elsewhere and was transient, compared with 30 per cent in the neighbouring Meath barony of Upper Moyfenrath. The larger proportion of outsiders in Carbury seems to indicate a continuing demand for farmworkers. There were many reasons why such employees relocated: some went to better positions; some emigrated; the death of an employee or his wife might cause a family to leave, as in the case of John James Hall, a coachman at Ballindoolin, whose young family was broken up after the death of his wife, Sarah in 1913.[9]

While the farmers of Carbury prospered during the First World War, as the prices for the food they produced increased a hundredfold, they did not raise their labourers' wages commensurately. Affected by a rising cost of living, and now represented by the Irish Transport and General Workers' Union, the farm labourers of Kildare joined a national campaign for improvements, which inevitably brought conflict with the Farmers' Union. A strike in the summer of 1919 led farmers to call on all able-bodied family members and to make a greater than usual effort to help each other bring in the harvest. The strike was ended with agreement on 32s. per week for six ten-hour days for men aged 20 and above and 26s. for younger men, with bonuses for Sunday work and at harvest.[10]

A letter written from Coolavacoose in September 1919 gives an interesting perspective. Commenting that 'John and I thinned all the turnips and made all the hay ourselves and had the corn all cut as well', he added:

> E. Tyrrell and J. du Boe helped us to stook and we helped them. We had lovely weather all the time and the corn all stood grand. We have it all in now ready for the mill. The agreement arrived at is 32s. per week for a man finding his own board and 16s. for a man like J. Keegan who is boarded so, as he was getting milk and plenty of other things for nothing (he was getting 15s. before the strike), he is not as well off, as John cut off all these things. They had pickets going about and stopped cattle on the road going to Dublin but were very quiet round here otherwise.[11]

Over the next few years, a weak economy and high unemployment enabled farmers to reduce the adult wage to 30s. and farm labourers fared badly.

Among the rare insights into the working of farms and the lives of the labourers are recollections by William Beatty and Paddy Mulrany about the Palmer estate at Rahan, both of which suggest a happy and prosperous farm. Beatty recalled that Charles Colley Palmer 'was a humble man who never wanted to own a motor car, he travelled by horse-drawn carriages with a man named John Robins doing the driving ... The big house itself used only paraffin oil for the lights ... the water supply to the house was very advanced for the time as water was pumped automatically by a ram which worked using no fuel, day after day ... A big indoor female staff was employed'. Many years later, Beatty could name the herdsmen, land steward, paymaster, cattle buyer, gamekeeper, gardener and many general farm workers, adding: 'Should cattle get sick, they would make up their own doses. No veterinary surgeons in those days'.[12] Beatty's recollections of homemade cures reflect the then-current practice, although in each generation there was always at least one farmer who was called on as unofficial vet.

Mulrany started work aged 13 on a local farm where the pay was £6 per year, with dinner and supper provided. When he secured a job as herd and general labourer at Rahan, he was paid 9*s.* per week without meals. He worked for the Palmers for about thirty years and recalled that there was always plenty of help to do the work, specifically remembering fourteen men finishing the last cock of hay one summer's evening. He also mentioned that many farm labourers had no winter work and made a sort of living by trapping rabbits. Records of the sale of rabbits and bonuses paid to the trappers are included in the Palmer accounts.[13] Clearly ordered and well written, they list and value all stock and potatoes, mangolds, hay, straw, oats and ensilage 'on hand' at the beginning of the year and record the prices at which animals were bought and sold at the various markets and fairs. Even the luck money was registered, as in an entry for 7 October 1919, recording the sale of twenty bullocks at Edenderry fair for £520, 'luck off: £2 10*s.*' A computation was made for 1919 of 'the weekly value of our own produce', counting two pigs killed for the house, poultry, eggs, milk, butter and potatoes but excluding vegetables and fruit produced in the garden. The farm machinery was also listed and valued, the most significant items being a binder, two mowing machines, two ploughs, two rakes, two harrows, six carts, a threshing mill and a corn drill. There is no hint in this volume that the farming routine was disturbed by political events. The Palmers were, of course, well aware of the upheaval caused by the First World War and the ongoing struggle for independence but it was as if nothing must disrupt the farming year. Such was Palmer's optimism that he built Rahan church on his estate in 1912.[14] Yet, within a few years, Rahan House became one of the casualties in twentieth-century Carbury. After the estate was purchased by the Irish Land Commission, the house was abandoned and its roof used to rebuild St Joseph's Orphanage in Co. Cavan after a disastrous fire in 1943. The estate is recalled affectionately by local poet, Dr Philip Brady, as

> a beautiful place …
> with its pleasure gardens,
> and a canal fed from the Boyne,
> where there would be small boats
> by the bridge in summer.[15]

Once the Civil War had ended, the Cumann na nGaedheal government quickly tried to solve the problems that Wyndham's Land Act did not address. While the cattle and sheep farmers had benefited most in becoming substantial landowners and small farmers had obtained a few extra acres, many of them still had less than fifteen acres. They and the landless labourers clamoured for land, whether from estates or from the bigger cattle farms. The 1923 Land Act gave the Irish Land Commission powers of compulsory purchase and redistribution and by 1941 more than 41,000 acres of Kildare had been redistributed, mostly from large estates, yet in 1957 nearly 60 per cent of holdings had a value of less than £15, rendering them 'uneconomic'.[16] The process subsequently affected smaller farms and left some owners with only a house and garden. While the redistribution programme completed the transfer of land to former tenants and enabled families from congested districts in the west of Ireland to settle in Kildare, it caused a lot of anger and left long-standing residual resentment. While Kevin Whelan's contention that

> the distribution of land with the avowed aim of getting as many Irish families as possible rooted in the soil of Ireland ... created at the heart of the farming system ... a conservatism which deemed the maintenance of the existing situation as the primary aim, and which was ill-equipped or inclined to make radical changes to accommodate to the changing circumstances of the second half of the twentieth century[17]

rings true, one may have reservations about it in the context of Carbury, where the farming community remained remarkably positive.

When the first Fianna Fáil government came to power in 1932, Taoiseach Éamon de Valera precipitated a land war over the 'land annuities' still payable to the British government. Britain quickly imposed a 20 per cent tariff on imports from the Irish Free State and retaliation by Ireland led to an economic war. While British trade, particular that of coal, suffered, Irish trade, which depended greatly on Britain, was crippled. As the cattle trade collapsed, live cattle were imported from Argentina, farmers suffered badly and the entire Irish economy was put under strain. In Carbury, big cattle farmers depended on the long-established system whereby most of their cattle went to the sales in Prussia Street, Dublin, and on to England by boat. Such farmers were seriously affected by the loss of trade and it took years to recover after the economic war ended.

While Carbury farmers regularly met at marts and creameries, the twentieth-century agricultural organizations became important in the farming community. In the years after the First World War, they were active in the Farmers' Union and the farmers of the next generation joined Macra na Feirme in the 1940s, welcoming its social outlets and young farmers' training initiatives. A local group was formed, the list of the committee for the local agricultural show in June 1955 reads as follows: 'K.R.E. Potterton (chairman), W. Bulfin and S.J. Holt (joint honorary secretaries), J. Pollard, J. McMahon, Brendan Foran, Henry Hill (Edenderry Y.F.C.), G.E.N. Clarke, R. Bourke, Frank Tyrrell, J. Broe, Thomas Tyrrell (Balyna and Carbury Y.F.C.)'.[18] In that year, Macra na Feirme members were to the fore in the foundation of the National Farmers' Association. Over the years, the Cadamstown/Carbury branch provided county chairmen, secretaries and representatives, national chairpersons and council representatives. Several of the 1955 show committee and others, such as Gordon Hickson and Hubert Potterton, were active in both the NFA and its successor, the Irish Farmers' Association.[19]

The IFA won the same support locally as the NFA and Carbury farmers served faithfully on county and national committees. One of these, A.K. (Sandy) Gallie, was a Scotsman, who came to Ireland after the Second World War. On securing a farm at Garrisker and marrying Joan Smith of Ballyhagan, he became deeply involved in the local community at Balyna and the parish of Carbury, was secretary of the Carbury branch of the IFA and later the Kildare treasurer. His son Roy continues to farm at Garrisker and is a prominent member of the IFA. Sam and Pearl Holt of Coolavacoose worked hard for both organizations. Looking back in 2005, Sam wrote:

> I am proud to have been in at the start of the foundation of the Irish Farmers' Association and to have been associated with so many dedicated people, irrespective of their religion or political background, who worked together for the betterment of people who … loved and worked the land.[20]

In the same article, he explained that 'in May 1955, we set out to canvass systematically every holding big and small to encourage people to join the NFA and point out the value of the united front'. The united front was needed in October 1966 when 30,000 farmers from every county in Ireland converged on Dublin as part of a farmers' rights march, to focus national attention on the difficult situation in the farming community. When the minister for agriculture declined to meet them, they spent twenty days and nights outside the Department of Agriculture. Finally, the government agreed to talks but little progress was made and in January 1967 members blocked bridges and roads, bringing traffic to a standstill. By the middle of May 1967 one hundred farmers had been jailed for non-payment of resultant fines and two thousand wives and daughters paraded in Portlaoise. In June 1967 all the prisoners were released and their homecoming was marked with much celebration. This action led to greater cohesion within the NFA and recognition of the importance of agricultural organizations in Irish economic life.

Pearl Holt was the first woman to chair an IFA national committee. She was one of a small number of farming women who were actively involved, particularly in issues such as farm health, safety and inheritance issues. Holt proved a gifted spokeswoman for farmers and their wives. In advance of Ireland's accession to the then European common market, she encouraged farmers' wives, who might soon be offering hospitality in farm guesthouses, to learn a European language. As always, Holt gave practical advice on how to set about a project.[21] Writing in the *Irish Farmers' Journal* in 1973, she urged Irish families to educate their daughters so that they could take their rightful place in Irish public life. 'This generation of mothers should never forget that we form half the electorate and should have a fair representation in the Dáil'.[22] An *Irish Press* article by Michael Sharkey in 1978, entitled 'Plea by Farm Wife', gave her an opportunity to counter urban criticism of farmers for rising food prices, using clear statistics to support her arguments.[23] Holt's clear and fluent speeches and articles are remarkable for the time, as women's voices were little heard. Another organization in which she and many local women were involved was the Irish Countrywomen's Association, founded in 1910 to improve health, education and living conditions for farming families and to encourage rural women to play a role in public life.

11. Ardkill House, built *c.*1820 by the Sale family, whose descendants, the Pottertons, still live there (by Rachel Clarke)

The Holts are a good example of a Church of Ireland farming family embedded in the local community but the position of Carbury parish was increasingly perilous and in the early 1980s there was a serious danger that the church might be closed. The parish treasurer, Arthur Tyrrell, led parishioners to accept amalgamation with Edenderry in return for a promise that Carbury church would remain open and it continues to serve the small Anglican community.

Several interviewees spoke about Carbury in terms of 'a soft and kind place'. While disputes arose between farmers from time to time, as in any agrarian community, neighbourliness generally prevailed and farmers long maintained the custom of keeping a few drills where their workers and neighbours could raise potatoes and other vegetables for their own use. For instance, Thomas Potterton and his son Hubert always gave a man grazing for a cow on the farm at Ardkill, whereby he could provide milk for his family (fig. 11). There was no charge made for this 'house cow' and the man even had his own gate by which he could come and go. Such acts of kindness were common but are virtually unrecorded.

The evolution of farming and society in Carbury depended on a number of factors. Its topography, climate and distance from Dublin or any other large conurbation have preserved it as a bastion of cattle and sheep rearing and the land still shows a pattern of holdings dating from the estates laid out in the sixteenth and seventeenth centuries. Those estates have long gone but many descendants of their erstwhile tenants still live on and farm the land.

Reviewing four centuries in the barony of Carbury, the most striking feature is the stability of the farming community. Through all the challenges of civil strife and famine, transition from tenancy to ownership, modernization and urban expansion, succeeding generations of farmers have sustained not only the land but a way of life rooted in the soil of Carbury. While much farmland along the main roads to Dublin has been sold for housing, the Carbury landscape remains firmly agricultural, as both long-established families and those who bought land in the twentieth century maintain the farming community in the heart of a richly fertile country.

Notes

CKAS	County Kildare Archaeological Society
Commons Jn. Ire.	*Journal of the House of Commons of the kingdom of Ireland*
cwt	hundredweight (*centum weight*)
HC	House of Commons
IFA	Irish Farmers' Association
IRA	Irish Republican Army
JCKAS	*Journal of the County Kildare Archaeological Society*
JP	Justice of the Peace
MU CSHIHE	Maynooth University, Centre for the Study of Historic Irish Houses and Estates
NAI	National Archives of Ireland
NFA	National Farmers' Association
NIAH	National Inventory of Architectural Heritage
NLI	National Library of Ireland
NUI	National University of Ireland
OMARC	Office of Public Works – Maynooth University Research Centre
PRONI	Public Record Office of Northern Ireland
RCB	Library of the Representative Church Body of the Church of Ireland
RD	Registry of Deeds
RHP	right-hand page
RIC	Royal Irish Constabulary
TCD	Trinity College Dublin
UCD	University College Dublin

INTRODUCTION

1 Matthew Devitt, 'Carbury and the Berminghams' country', *JCKAS*, 2 (1896), pp 85–111; Walter FitzGerald, 'Two Colley inscriptions in the Castle Carbury churchyard; with notes on the founder of the family', *JCKAS*, 8 (1917), pp 369–87; Karina Holton, 'Carbury, Co. Kildare, 1744–1911' in Karina Holton, Liam Clare and Brian Ó Daláigh (eds), *Irish villages: studies in local history* (Dublin, 2004), pp 96–130.

2 W.E. Vaughan, *Landlords and tenants in mid-Victorian Ireland* (Oxford, 1994).

3 William Nolan and Thomas McGrath (eds), *Kildare history and society* (Dublin, 2006).

4 In the Public Record Office in 1922,

in house fires or in clearances after the sale of the property or due to lack of continuity of solicitors' firms or even deliberate destruction.

5 J.H. Tyrrell, *A genealogical history of the Tyrrell family* (Twickenham, 1904).

6 NLI P.7214, Farm records of the Boylan family of Coonough, Co. Kildare.

7 J.C. Duggan, *250 years at Highfield: a short history of the Duggan family* (Carbury, 1997).

8 RD 89/282/63209, lease, 13 Aug. 1737.

9 RCB P.0524.01/2 Carbury combined register, 1828–48.

10 MU CSHIHE, Holt Papers (the property of Mrs Pearl Holt, on permanent loan), Holt farm journal, 1798–1879.

11 Neither Methodists nor Presbyterians ever had a church in the barony.

12 Terence Dooley, 'IRA activity in Kildare during the War of Independence' in Nolan and McGrath (eds), *Kildare history and society*, pp 625–56; Ciarán Reilly, 'Like shooting snipe at Ballindoolin: William Upton Tyrrell and the Great War' in Terence Dooley and Christopher Ridgway (eds), *The country house and the Great War: Irish and British experiences* (Dublin, 2016), pp 178–88.

1. CARBURY BEFORE 1700

1   NLI MS 9212, M.J. Byrn, Maps of the estate of the Misses Colley in the barony of Carbury, Co. Kildare, 1744.
2   *Fiants Ire.*, Hen. VIII, no. 442, Nov. 1544.
3   F.H.A. Aalen, 'The Irish rural landscape: synthesis of habitat and history' in F.H.A. Aalen, Kevin Whelan and Matthew Stout (eds), *Atlas of the Irish rural landscape* (Cork, 1997), pp 4–30 at p. 23.
4   Henry Colley to Salmon, lease, 22 Dec. 1691, recited in RD 18/231/8918, 20 June 1715.
5   NLI Betham's genealogical abstracts of prerogative wills, old series, x, p. 17.

2. THE EIGHTEENTH CENTURY: WITHIN THE COLLEY ESTATE

1   He was the grandfather of the duke of Wellington.
2   Byrn, Maps, 1744. His numbering of holdings is so chaotic and his failure to ensure that the pages of the report were bound in correct order make it unfeasible to include specific references.
3   Sarah Bendall, *Dictionary of land surveyors and local map makers of Great Britain and Ireland* (London, 1997).
4   TCD MS Deposit Armytage, A booke of maps of the estate of the Right Honourable the earl of Mountrath in the kingdom of Ireland taken *anno domini* 1730.
5   John Andrews, 'The French School of Dublin land surveyors', *Irish Geography*, 5 (1967), pp 275–92 at p. 280.
6   As late as 1836, a district north and east of Longwood was detached and reassigned to Co. Meath. The townlands of Blackditch, Derrinlig and Freagh and part of Longwood were transferred from the barony of Carbury to the barony

of Upper Moyfenrath by Act 6 and 7, William IV.
7   Colley to Salmon, lease, 22 Dec. 1691.
8   RD 22/492/12670, assignment of lease, Salmon to Hurst, 23 Jan. 1718/19.
9   RD 155/342/104941, partition by lease and release, 18–19 Oct. 1752.
10 Prerogative Court of Canterbury wills, 1783. Probate of will of Joshua Glover, 14 Feb. 1783; probate of will of Elizabeth Glover, 3 Dec. 1813.
11 RD 127/351/87048, 6–7 Oct. 1747, Elizabeth and Mary Colley to the Incorporated Society, lease and release in perpetuity of 20 acres Irish plantation measure on the east side of Carbury Castle: see Kenneth Milne, *The Irish charter schools, 1730–1830* (Dublin, 1997).
12 RD 281/490/187638, 20 July 1771.
13 In 1752 Elizabeth and Mary Colley had preserved to themselves the right to nominate and appoint vicars (RD 155/342/10494) but such rights lapsed at the time of the disestablishment of the Church of Ireland in 1870.
14 Incorporated Society in Dublin for Promoting (English) Protestant Schools in Ireland, Board book, TCD 5236, 25 Nov. 1772.
15 *Commons Jn. Ire.*, xii, part iii, p. dcccxx: TCD 5239, 20 Dec. 1786.
16 By 1794, approximately 159 girls had been apprenticed: *Samuel Watson's gentleman's and citizen's almanack* (Dublin, 1794), p. 81.
17 TCD 5243, 27 July 1796.
18 TCD 5228, 6 Apr. 1803, a view supported by the Rebellion Papers, 1797, 620/30/36–8 (NAI).
19 TCD 5227, 6 June 1798; Rebellion Papers, 1797, 620/32/77; *Commons Jn. Ire.*, 19, p. ccxii.
20 In 1813, Harberton gave the lands that had belonged to the charter school to the Church of Ireland as glebe lands. PRONI T2954/8/33, Harberton Papers. The grant was confirmed in February 1824 (RD 798/441/539176).
21 NLI PC 12467, list of persons who have suffered losses on their property in the county of Kildare, 1799.
22 Garrett Tyrrell made no claim for losses.
23 Patrick J. Duffy, 'The territorial identity of Kildare's landscapes' in Nolan and

McGrath (eds), *Kildare history and society*, pp 1–34 at pp 28–9.

24 Alexander Taylor's 1783 map of the County of Kildare, available at digitalarchive.mcmaster.ca/islandora/object/macrepo%3A92714 (accessed 3 Dec. 2022). The survey of Kildare buildings by the NIAH was done many years ago and is far from complete. A further survey, with a review of the original dating of houses, is planned.

25 Will of John Boylan, 2 June 1796, photocopy in NLI P.7214 Boylan Papers.

3. THE EIGHTEENTH CENTURY: OUTSIDE THE COLLEY ESTATE

1 RD 3/353/1064, lease and release, 16–17 Mar. 1709/10, Bellew to Joseph Leeson et al. As a supporter of Charles I, Richard's father, Sir John Bellew, had forfeited his lands in Cromwell's time but had recovered them under Charles II. He had lands in Carbury through his marriage to Mary Bermingham, daughter of Walter.

2 Lease, 1 Nov. 1692, recited in RD 8/414/3033, mortgage, 29–30 May 1712, Dudley Colley et al. to Richard Fenner.

3 Will printed in Temple Prime, *Some account of the Palmer family of Rahan, Co. Kildare, Ireland* (New York, 1903), fourth edition, pp 28–9.

4 RD 114/162/78429, lease of town and lands of Ballinderry for lives, renewable for ever, Josiah Hort to William Tyrrell, Kilrainy, 14 May 1743. The original is Ballinderry Papers, MS 1.

5 RD 22/24/11217, mortgage, 26–7 May 1718.

6 See, for instance, *Dublin Evening Post*, 23 Dec. 1790.

7 RD 34/347/21864, assignment, 22 Aug. 1772, endorsed on a lease of 12 Nov. 1703, William Sherlock, Co. Westmeath, to James Mills, Clonmeen, for forty-one years.

8 RD 7/175/2057, lease, Henry Colley to John Barcroft, 31 Jan. 1710/11.

9 RD 13/51/4916, lease for lives to William Smith, 7 Jan. 1709/10; RD 13/54/4918, lease for lives to Thomas Jackson, 7 Jan. 1709/10, of lands in Drehid.

10 Among the families with whom the Smiths intermarried in the nineteenth century were the Clarkes, du Boes,

Fawcetts and Sales. Drehid passed down through generations of the Smiths to Frances, who married Charles Kerr Douglas in 1901, and hence to Alan Douglas in this generation.

11 See Albert Cook Myers, *Immigration of Irish Quakers into Pennsylvania, 1682–1750* (Swarthmore, PA, 1901).

12 Her mother's will, 23 Apr. 1732, included a legacy to Ann in Pennsylvania. P. Beryl Eustace and Olive C. Goodbody (eds), *Quaker records, Dublin: abstracts of wills* (Dublin, 1957), no. 182.

13 An example is the will (RD 36/23/380) of Charles Mallowny, a Colley tenant at Ballyhagan, who left his estate in 1713 to his wife, Catherine, 'during her widowhood' only, with reversion to his nephew.

14 RD 306/405/203865, 23 Jan. 1772.

15 RD 306/202/203056, 19 Oct. 1774. His sons were to pay him £800 and an annuity.

16 The Tyrrell accounts, 1777–80, show large sums being spent at the Ballinasloe fair.

17 Richard Twiss, *A tour in Ireland in 1775* (London, 1776), p. 30.

18 Mill established by Edward Wolstenholme, tenant and later owner of Newberry Hall. The Pilkingtons, who bought Newberry Hall from him, converted the mill to the production of paper but closed it *c.*1881.

19 *Commons Jn. Ire.*, xviii, p. 149; *Commons Jn. Ire.*, xxix, p. 100.

20 The originals of the Civil Survey, 1654–66, were destroyed in a fire in 1711 but copies of the returns for ten counties survived. VIII, County of Kildare, is available online on the Irish Manuscripts Commission website as a digital edition. The Down Survey maps are also available on the TCD website. http://downsurvey.tcd.ie/1641-depositions.php.

21 NIAH no. 11801014.

22 RD 1/229/138, lease, Bellew to Medcalf, 16 Oct. 1708; RD 83/332/59132, lease, 29 July 1736.

23 Moorestown was part of the Kildare estate of the King family of Boyle.

24 Map of the separate parks of Williamstown by Nick Moran, 1770,

Ballindoolin Papers, OMARC, PP/
BAL/22/6.

25 Ballindoolin Papers, PP/BAL/22/2.

26 NIAH no. 11900308.

4. THE NINETEENTH CENTURY: BEFORE AND
AFTER THE GREAT FAMINE

1 See Karen Harvey, *The Bellews of
Mount Bellew: a Catholic gentry family in
eighteenth-century Ireland* (Dublin,1998);
Ciaran O'Neill, *Catholics of consequence:
transnational education, social mobility and
the Irish Catholic elite, 1850–1900* (Oxford,
2014).

2 The family's involvement in the estate
was diminished after his death in 1911
and in 1960, it was sold to the Bewley
family as a farm to supply its cafés
in Dublin. Sold again in 1983, it was
converted to the Moyvalley Hotel and
Golf Club.

3 Two books of workmen's accounts, for
1822 and 1825, give their names, days
worked, wages and details of the exact
job on any given day. PP/BAL/ 17/1–4.

4 PRONI, T2954/6/2, Harberton Papers,
letter, 10 June 1799, Tyrawley to
Harberton.

5 MU, CSHIHE, will of John Holt
(1729–1804), 16 Nov. 1801.

6 MU, CSHIHE, Holt Papers, Holt
farm journal, 1798–1879; transcript on
CKAS website. See Lesley Whiteside,
'The farm journal of the Holt family of
Coolavacoose, Carbury, Co. Kildare,
1798–1879', *JCKAS*, 23 (2020–1), pp
194–209. Coolavacoose was considered
part of Oldcourt in 1744.

7 Holt farm journal, 1798–1879, RHP
unmarked (page lxiii).

8 Lease in the possession of David W.J.
Clarke; map by G. Hevey.

9 RCB vestry minute books, 1797–1988,
P.524.5.1–6; registers of vestrymen,
1870–1993, P.524.6.1–2; combined
register of baptisms, 1804–29, marriages,
1805–27, burials 1805–29, P.524.1.1;
combined register of baptisms, 1828–47,
marriages, 1829–45, burials, 1828–48,
P.524.1.2, register of baptisms, 1847–
1902, P.524.2, register of marriages,
1845–1918, P.524.3, register of burials,
1848–1911, P.524.4.

10 The Roman Catholic marriage records
do not indicate the residence of *both*
bride and groom.

11 Civil registration records, district of
Edenderry, 1870–5.

12 Special parish cesses for the poor were
often levied in addition to the regular
parish cess, which was levied annually to
cover day-to-day costs.

13 RCB P.524.1.1, vestry minutes, 7 Apr.
1810.

14 William Dudley Wodsworth (ed.), *A brief
history of the ancient Foundling Hospital of
Dublin, from the year 1702* (Dublin, 1876).

15 RCB P.524.7.1.

16 A letter of the alphabet was given to
each year, a system also used by livestock
farmers. Thanks to Mark Roe for
sharing information from his M.Phil.
thesis, 'The Foundling Hospital: origins
and outcomes', TCD, 2019.

17 RCB P.524.3, register of marriages, 1845–
1918; RCB P.524.1.1, combined register.
It is doubtful that Ellen was a foundling,
for an Ellen McKenny, daughter of
Robert and Hannah of Carbury, was
baptized in Carbury in 1818.

18 Note book of Charles Lindsay recording
his episcopal visitations in the diocese of
Kildare, 1804–8, RCB MS 8, p. 102, 23
July 1808. See also Raymond Refaussé's
edition, in *JCKAS*, 17 (1989–91), pp
121–47.

19 RCB MS 8, unnumbered final page.

20 Ibid., pp 103–4.

21 Ibid., pp 54 and 125.

22 Ibid., p. 114.

23 Ibid., p. 119.

24 Holt family journal, 1798–1879.

25 Approximately three million in 1700,
between four and five million in 1800,
more than eight million at the time
of the 1841 census. The first national
census was held in 1821 with subsequent
censuses every ten years but almost
all the returns for 1821 to 1851 were
destroyed in the Four Courts in 1922,
those for 1861 and 1871 were destroyed
soon after the census was taken and those
for 1881 and 1891 were pulped during
the First World War due to the shortage
of paper. Only the statistics survive for
censuses before 1901.

26 *Report from the commissioners of the board of education in Ireland, eleventh report, parish schools*, HC 1813–14, pp 273ff.

27 The report, not published at the time, was printed with the report of the Kildare commission. See *Evidence taken before her majesty's commissioners of enquiry into the state of the endowed schools in Ireland*, HC 1857–8, 341–79.

28 *Report from the commissioners of the board of education in Ireland, fourteenth report, view of the chief foundations, with some general remarks and result of deliberations*, HC 1813–14 (21), vi.

29 Regulations of the Society for Promoting the Education of the Poor in Ireland, fourth annual report, 1816.

30 See Susan Parkes, *Kildare Place: the history of the Church of Ireland Training College, 1811–1969* (Dublin, 1984).

31 The sixteenth report of the Society for Promoting the Education of the Poor in Ireland (Dublin, 1828, pp 50–1, 94, 113) recorded forty-three scholars. Clonkeen schoolhouse still stands.

32 NAI ED 1/43, no. 39.

33 See Donald Akenson, *The Irish education experiment* (London, 1970); John Coolahan, *Irish education, its history and structure* (Dublin, 1981); Brendan Walsh, *Essays in the history of Irish education* (London, 2016).

34 Royal Commission of Inquiry into Primary Education in Ireland, HC 1870, 28, part 3, questions 8233–9.

35 Brendan Grimes, 'Funding a Roman Catholic church in nineteenth-century Ireland', *Architectural History*, 52 (2009), pp 147–66.

36 My thanks to Oliver Conlan for drawing my attention to the significance of these statistics and for the loan of his BA thesis, 'The barony of Carbury, Co. Kildare, from pre-Famine through land agitation and the break-up of the estates' (NUI, Maynooth, 2008).

37 William Nolan, 'The land of Kildare: valuation, ownership and occupation, 1850–1906' in Nolan and McGrath (eds), *Kildare history and society*, pp 549–84 at p. 569.

38 *Report from her majesty's commissioners of inquiry into the state of the law and practice in respect to the occupation of land in Ireland. Minutes of evidence*, part 3, HC 1845, hereafter *Devon Commission*, part 3, evidence of Richard Grattan M.D. (1001), question 48, p. 656. The evidence of Robert Rawson (969), question 47, p. 578, painted a similar picture.

39 PRONI, *Letters of a great Irish landlord: a selection from the estate correspondence of the 3rd marquess of Downshire, 1809–45* (Belfast, 1974), no. 55.

40 Ciarán Reilly, *Edenderry, 1820–1920: popular politics and Downshire rule* (Dublin, 2007), pp 36–40.

41 Cess was fixed each year by the county grand jury (made up of local large landowners). The system was open to corruption and was eventually abolished by the Local Government Act of 1898.

42 RCB P.524.5.1, vestry minutes, 17 Apr. 1882.

43 NAI, Relief Commission Papers RLFC 2/Z565021, 3/1, 1126, 30 Mar. 1846.

44 See Karel Kiely, 'Poverty and famine in Co. Kildare, 1820 to 1850' in Nolan and McGrath (eds), *Kildare history and society*, pp 493–534.

45 Kildare Lent Assizes, 1847. *Dublin Weekly Nation*, 3 Apr. 1847.

46 *Freeman's Journal*, 1 June 1886.

47 Kevin Whelan, 'The modern landscape: from plantation to present' in Aalen, Whelan and Stout (eds), *Atlas of the Irish rural landscape*, pp 67–103 at p. 89.

48 Devon Commission, part 3, evidence of Richard Grattan, p. 656.

49 An active Carbury parishioner, his tombstone states that he served as medical officer for forty-eight years. He lived in Derrinturn House.

50 Charles Payne and Joseph Payne had 174 and 160 acres respectively; Thomas Clarke, Edward Kenny and Thomas Tyrrell each had more than 50 acres.

51 Anne Clarke, Thomas Clarke, Richard McCann and Thomas O'Brien each had more than 50 acres in Kishavanna Upper, as had Thomas Bennett, James Dunne and Mary Fitzsimon in Kishavanna Lower.

52 *The Warder* of 2 Mar. 1861 reported a state reception at which Mrs Holt wore a 'train and corsage of the richest black moire antique … and a coronet of pearls, lappets and court plumes'.

53 Lease, 1 Feb. 1805, Elizabeth Glover to Andrew Mullowney for twenty-one years of 100 acres 'of that part of Clonmeen commonly called Highfield', printed in Duggan, *250 years at Highfield*, p. 49.

54 Duggan, *250 years at Highfield*, p. 30.

55 Homan Potterton, *Potterton people and places* (Drogheda, 2006), p. 56. They later built two more houses, at Coolcor and Clonmeen. All three faced Carbury Castle.

5. THE NINETEENTH CENTURY: LAND REFORM

1 Holt farm journal, 1798–1879; NLI P.7214, farm account book of J. Boylan of Coonagh, c.1853–1916. See also farm account book, 1824–83 (NLI P.7214); Duggan, *250 years at Highfield*.

2 *The Irish Farmers' Gazette*, 8 Apr. 1869.

3 *The Evening Freeman*, 30 Oct. 1869. He later described himself as agent for the Dublin and Wicklow Manure Company, Clonkeen, Edenderry and Robertstown (*Freeman's Journal*, 10 Sept. 1874).

4 Tenants could borrow two thirds of the purchase money from the government and repay it at 5 per cent over thirty-five years.

5 Holt versus Viscount Harberton, Naas Land Sessions, 10 Apr. 1871. For verdict, see Francis Nolan and Robert Romney Kane, *The statutes relating to the law of landlord and tenant in Ireland since 1860* (Dublin, 1974), pp 406–11. Reported in the *Irish Builder*, 15 Apr. 1871 and *Freeman's Journal*, 10 Jan. 1872.

6 W.E. Vaughan, *Landlords and tenants in mid-Victorian Ireland*, p. 94.

7 See the entry for Judge William Grattan Holt, his son, in Frank W. Blackmar (ed.), *Kansas: a cyclopaedia of state history* (Chicago, IL, 1912), 3, part 1, pp 619–20.

8 RD 1873/11/112, sale, 21 Mar. 1873, of Samuel Holt's interest in Haggard to Frederick Pilkington; RD 1875/6/117. Carbury House became the vicarage, later the rectory.

9 *Landowners in Ireland, accounts and papers*, 39, 1876, 80, pp 27–34.

10 Francis Metcalf, for instance, bought 145 acres of the earl of Milltown's land in Dunfierth under the Encumbered Estates Act.

11 Fee farm grant, 14 Oct. 1857, recited in RD 1889/36/232.

12 *Kildare Observer*, 28 May 1881.

13 *Leinster Leader*, 25 June 1881. Fr Wyer and other Roman Catholic clergy were also prominent at the Carbury sheriff's sale.

14 Ciarán Reilly, 'Like shooting snipe at Ballindoolin', p. 178. Willie Tyrrell's diaries, 1883–1915, at PP/BAL/44/350–367 and 45/368–383.

15 Letter, 16 Oct. 1886, printed in Duggan, *250 years at Highfield*, p. 57.

16 RD 1888/8/225, 226, 229. The cost of purchase, depending on the land and the particular lease that a tenant had, was typically between £13 and £23 per acre.

17 The purchasing tenant received a land certificate of registration of title in fee simple. David Clarke still has Richard Clarke's certificate for 35 acres at Coolavacoose. His registration appears with those of Samuel Holt, Coolavacoose, Thomas Potterton, Ardkill, William Smith, Collinstown and Richard McCann, Clonkeen, in the records of the Registry of Deeds.

18 *Leinster Leader*, 18 July 1885.

19 *Kildare Observer*, 29 June 1889.

20 *Leinster Leader*, 29 June 1889.

21 An example was Charles Smith, son of John and Jane of Clonmeen, an unmarried millionaire merchant in the United States. A copy of his will of 15 June 1888 is in the possession of Roy Gallie.

22 The Loucks and Clarke Corporation, undated printed prospectus, copy in possession of David Clarke.

6. THE TWENTIETH CENTURY: ORGANIZATION AND GROWTH

1 *The Kildare Observer*, 18 July 1914.

2 Reported in *Leinster Leader*, 28 Aug. 1916.

3 All were recorded on a war memorial scroll, dedicated at an ecumenical Remembrance service in Carbury church in 2019.

4 De Ruvigny's Roll of Honour, 1914–18, 2, p. 222. Letter, Dr Philip Brady to LW, 14 Oct. 2022.

5 Reilly, 'Like shooting snipe', pp 184–5.

6 UCD, Mulcahy Papers, P7a/6.

7   Terence Dooley, 'IRA activity in Kildare during the War of Independence', pp 630–1.

8   See Terence Dooley, *Burning the big house: the story of the Irish country house in a time of war and revolution* (New Haven, 2022) and Lesley Whiteside, 'Church of Ireland parish and people in Westmeath, 1897–1996' in William Nolan and Seamus O'Brien (eds), *Westmeath history and society* (Dublin, 2022), pp 551–75.

9   Gertrude and George were sent to the Bird's Nest Home, Kingstown (Dún Laoghaire), where most of the children were trained for domestic service. Their younger sister, Olivia, was sent to the Cottage Home for Little Children, Kingstown. The extent of the breakup of the family is illustrated by the fact that in 1914, she went to live in Philadelphia with her aunt and was followed by her sister.

10   See Tom Nelson, 'A stand-up fight: the conflict between farmers and farm labourers in Kildare in 1919', *JCKAS*, 23 (2020–1), pp 120–35.

11   Holt Papers, photocopy of letter, 21 Sept. 1919, unknown author (probably a brother of Edward) to Edward Holt (abroad).

12   William Beatty, 'The Palmer estate of Rahan', *Balyna Annual*, 1986, pp 30–1.

13   'Is he Balyna's oldest resident?', *Balyna Annual*, 1978, p. 27; Palmer estate farm account book, 1918–33, PP/BAL/17/5.

14   It may have been an admirable act of devotion but the building of an estate church ignored the developing situation within the Church of Ireland nationally. During the twentieth century, it became increasingly obvious that it had more churches than it could maintain and as congregations dwindled, many churches closed. Rahan church finally closed in the 1980s.

15   Philip Brady, 'Palmer's house' in *Missing* (Edenderry, 2012).

16   Terence Dooley, *The land for the people: the land question in independent Ireland* (Dublin, 2004), p. 137. See also Evan Comerford, 'Land distribution and migration to Kildare in the post-independence era', *JCKAS*, 23 (2020–1), pp 152–68.

17   Whelan, 'The modern landscape: from plantation to present', p. 98.

18   *Leinster Leader*, 4 June 1955.

19   The Holts kept scrapbooks relating to these farming organizations (Holt Papers).

20   Sam Holt, article in a supplement celebrating fifty years of the Kildare/West Wicklow IFA, *Leinster Leader*, 7 Apr. 2005.

21   'French spoke here', *Irish Farmers' Journal*, 7 June 1972.

22   'What's wrong with us women?', *Irish Farmers' Journal*, 6 Jan. 1973.

23   *Irish Press*, 9 Dec. 1978.

Index

Act of Settlement 13, 14
Act of Union 49
Agriculture, Department of 78
Angier, William (*fl.* 1804) 49
Ardkill, Co. Kildare 12, 13, 19, 22, 31, 58, 60, 79
Argentina 76
Armagh, Co. 31
Armit family 66
Australia 68, 69

Ballinakill Lower, Co. Kildare 65
Ballinasloe, Co. Galway 35, 83
Ballinderry, Co. Kildare 7, 11, 13, 25, 29, 30, 41, 66
Ballindoolin, Co. Kildare 7, 13, 31, 61, 70
Ballitore, Co. Kildare 31, 32
Ballyboy, Co. Offaly 40
Ballybrack, Co. Kildare 65
Ballyburly, Co. Offaly 48
Ballygibbon East, Co. Kildare 57, 58, 67, 68
Ballygibbon West, Co. Kildare 57, 67, 68
Ballyhagan, Co. Kildare 11, 20, 68, 77, 83
Ballykean, Co. Offaly 49
Ballymorane, Co. Offaly 31
Ballynadrumny, Co. Kildare 41
Ballyonan, Co. Kildare 38
Ballyvane, Co. Kildare 11, 22
Balyna, Co. Kildare 8, 9, 11, 13, 19, 28, 37, 43, 61, 77
Balyna and Carbury Young Farmers' Club 77
Barcroft, Alice (1684–1732) 40–1
Barcroft, John (1664–1723) 31
Barcroft, Thomas (*fl.* 1708) 40
Barcroft, William (1612–96) 31
Beatty, William (1913–) 74
Bell, William (*fl.* 1820) 48
Bellew family 28
Bellew, John, 1st baron of Duleek (–1693) 28
Bellew, Mary, née Bermingham (–1694) 83
Bellew, Richard, 3rd baron of Duleek (*c.*1671–1716) 28, 31, 40
Bennett, Hugh (*c.*1834–1902) 68

Bennett, Thomas (*fl.* 1853) 85
Berkeley, John, 4th Viscount Fitzhardinge of Berehaven (1650–1712) 28
Bermingham family 7, 11, 61
Bermingham, Mary (–1694) 83
Bermingham, Walter (–1638) 30
Bible 51
Birr, Co. Offaly 30
Blackditch, Co. Meath 82
Blessington, Co. Wicklow 18
Bor family 7, 30, 70
Bor, Ada (*c.*1860–1933) 72
Bor, Charlotte (1857–1933) 70
Bor, Edward (*c.*1817–70) 70
Bor, Humphrey (–1768) 31, 61, 70
Bor, William Loftus (1849–1914) 65
Bourke, R. (*fl.* 1955) 77
Boylan family 8, 59, 62
Boylan, Edward (*fl.* 1797) 27
Boylan, James (*fl.* 1744) 22
Boylan, James (*fl.* 1797) 27
Boylan, James (*fl.* 1853) 66
Boylan, John (–1797) 27
Boylan, Patrick (*fl.* 1797) 27
Boyle, Co. Roscommon 13
Boyne, river 11, 20, 75
Brady, Philip (1942–) 75
Brereton, John (*fl.* 1744) 21
Broadford, Co. Kildare 52
Broe, J. (*fl.* 1955) 77
Brookville, Co. Kildare 27, 65, 72
Brownrigg, James (*c.*1780–1817) 53
Bulfin, William (1919–88) 77
Byrn, Moses (*fl.* 1744) 16–22
Byrne, surveyor (*fl.* 1735) 16

Cadamstown, Co. Kildare 9
Calfstown, Co. Kildare 28
Canada 55, 68
Carbury Castle 11, 12, 13, 17, 82
Carbury Cricket Club 69
Carbury Hill 17, 24, 68
Carey family 60
Carlow, county 43
Carrick, Co. Kildare 7, 29, 31, 39, 48

Carter, Wesley (*c.*1974–) 44
Carton, Co. Kildare 18
Casey, Laurence (*fl.* 1830) 62
Castleknock, Co. Dublin 7
Castlejordan, Co. Meath 66
Castletown, Co. Kildare 7, 9
Catholic University of Ireland 9
Cave, William (*fl.* 1771) 24
Chandley, Benjamin (1685–1745) 32
Chandley, William (–1723) 32
Charles II, king (1630–85) 13
Church Education Society 50, 51
Church of England 12
Church of Ireland 12, 23–4, 46, 51, 69
Civil Survey, 1654 39, 65
Civil War 73, 76
Clarke family 26, 46, 61
Clarke, Ellen (*c.*1845–87) 68
Clarke, George Edward Newenham, alias
    Aden (1919–92) 77
Clarke, Henry (1884–) 68
Clarke, John (1868–1939) 68
Clarke, Richard (*c.*1824–1908) 68
Clarke, Richard (1870–) 68–9
Clarke, Thomas (1866–1915) 68, 85
Clarke, William (*fl.* 1825) 46
Clarke, William (1865–) 67
Clogherinkoe, Co. Kildare 52
Clonard, Co. Meath 39
Clonard Bridge, Co. Kildare 18, 30
Clonbullogue, Co. Offaly 46
Clonkeen, Co. Kildare 11, 19, 20, 38, 46, 50,
    51, 58, 63, 68, 69, 85
Clonkeeran, Co. Kildare 27
Clonmeen, Co. Kildare 27, 57, 83, 86
Coates, Thomas (*fl.* 1744) 21
Coffey family 58
Coffey, Patrick (*fl.* 1744) 19
Colley family 12, 13, 15, 16–17, 18, 19, 21–2,
    23, 24, 29, 43, 44, 65, 67
Colley, Charles (–1771) 28
Colley, Dudley (*fl.* 1734) 29
Colley, Elizabeth (–*c.*1813) 18–19, 20, 23, 24
Colley, George (–1615) 12
Colley, George (*fl.* 1692) 28, 29
Colley, George F. (1797–1879) 53
Colley, Sir Henry (–1584) 11, 12
Colley, Henry (–1601) 12
Colley, Henry (–1700) 14
Colley, Henry (–1724) 15
Colley, Henry (–*c.*1725) 15
Colley, Henry F. (1827–86) 66
Colley, Mary (*fl.* 1708) 28–9
Colley, Mary, née Hamilton (*fl.* 1731) 15, 19

Colley, Mary (*fl.* 1764) 18–19, 20, 23
Colley, Richard (*c.*1690–1758) 21, 28
Collinstown, Co. Kildare 58
Conolly family 9
Coolagh, Co. Kildare 63
Coolavacoose, Co. Kildare 8, 9, 11, 13, 22,
    26, 44–5, 49, 57, 59, 62, 74, 77, 84
Coolcor, Co. Kildare 20, 58, 86
Coolgreany, Co. Kildare 14, 58
Coonagh, Co. Kildare 13, 14, 22, 27, 57, 58,
    62–3
Cope family 48
Cope, James (*fl.* 1846) 48
Cork, county 73
Cramer, John (*fl.* 1744) 20
Cromwell, Oliver (1599–1658) 13
Cuffe, James, 1st baron of Tyrawley (–1724)
    44
Cumann na nGaedheal 76

Dáil Éireann 78
Daniel, Edward (*fl.* 1777) 38
Delahide, Sir Walter (*fl.* 1544) 11
Dempsey family 61
Dempsey, Patrick (*fl.* 1737) 9
Derrinlig, Co. Meath 82
Derrinturn, Co. Kildare 22, 46, 50, 52, 54,
    71, 85
Derryart, Co. Kildare 11, 22
de Valera, Éamon (1882–1975) 76
Devon Commission 52–3
Diggen family 58
Douglas family 32
Dowdall family 58
Dowdall, Christopher (*fl.* 1744) 20, 21
Dowdall, Joseph (*c.*1817–71) 63
Downside School, England 43
Drehid, Co. Kildare 27, 28, 32, 83
Drummin, Co. Kildare 13, 22, 25, 27,
    60–1
Dublin, city 14, 15, 18, 22, 24, 30, 34–5,
    37–8, 43, 46, 47, 56, 72, 76–7, 78
Dublin Castle 59
du Boe family 58, 83
du Boe, Henry (*fl.* 1744) 20
du Boe, Joseph (1875–1934) 74
Duggan family 8, 60, 61
Duggan, Denis (–1872) 57–8
Duggan, Francis (*fl.* 1744) 21
Duggan, Patrick (*fl.* 1838) 60
Duggan, Patrick (*fl.* 1886) 67
Dunfierth, Co. Kildare 24, 40–1, 86
Dunne, James (*fl.* 1853) 85
Dysart, Co. Kildare 28

Earle, Edward (*c*.1764–1846) 50
Easter Rising 72
Edenderry, Co. Offaly 12, 14, 20, 28, 31, 34, 46, 53, 56, 71, 75, 79
Edenderry Board of Guardians 54
Edenderry Poor–Law Union 53
Edenderry Young Farmers' Club 77
Elizabeth I, queen (1533–1603) 43
Encumbered Estates Act, 1849 56, 65, 86
Enfield, Co. Meath 56
England 34, 35, 68, 71, 77

Farmers' Union 73, 77
Farrell, John (*fl.* 1869) 63
Fawcett family 83
Fayle, William (*fl.* 1719) 22
Fenner, Richard (*fl.* 1712) 83
Fertullagh, Co. Westmeath 7
Fianna Fáil 76
First World War 71, 73, 75, 77
FitzGerald, Thomas, 10th earl of Kildare (1513–37) 11
Fitzpatrick, Sir Jeremiah (*c*.1740–1810) 24
Fitzsimon, Mary (*fl.* 1853) 85
Flanagan, Francis (*fl.* 1822) 45
Flanagan, James (*fl.* 1853) 58
Flinn family 58
Flinn, Christopher (*fl.* 1744) 58
Flinn, Patrick (*fl.* 1719) 22
Foran, Brendan (*fl.* 1955) 77
Ford House, Co. Kildare 22
Foundling Hospital, Dublin 46–7
France 34
Freagh, Co. Kildare 21, 58
Freagh, Co. Meath 82

Gaffney, John (*c*.1800–1880) 65
Gallie family 32
Gallie, Alexander Knox (1922–2005) 77
Gallie, Joan, née Smith (1922–96) 77
Gallie, Roy (1955–) 77, 86
Galway, county 35
Garrisker, Co. Kildare 11, 65, 77
Geashill, Co. Offaly 48
Gladstone, William Ewart (1809–98) 52, 63–4, 69
Glover, Joshua (–*c*.1783) 23
Gorteen, Co. Kildare 13, 40–1
Gough, Lieutenant George (*fl.* 1798) 25
Grand Canal 39
Grange, Co. Kildare 7, 13, 25, 30, 33, 34, 39, 59
Grattan family 14, 22, 27, 57, 58, 61
Grattan, Ann (1784–1853) 59

Grattan, Esther (–1798) 25
Grattan, John (1713–1787) 14, 59
Grattan, John (*fl.* 1744) 21
Grattan, John (1788–1836) 14
Grattan, Mary (–1798) 25
Grattan, Richard (1759–1839) 25
Grattan, Richard (1790–1886) 52–3, 54, 65
Grattan, Richard (1831–1846) 54
Grattan, Robert (*fl.* 1744) 21
Grattan, Simon (–1697) 14
Grattan, Thomas (1749–1801) 14
Great Famine 31, 46, 53–6, 59, 62, 68
Greenhill, Co. Offaly 48
Griffith, Sir Richard (1784–1878) 8, 57, 66

Haggard, Co. Kildare 20, 58–9, 60, 64–5, 86
Hall, George (1904–) 87
Hall, Gertrude (1900–98) 87
Hall, John James (*c*.1860–) 73
Hall, Olivia (1905–1929) 87
Hall, Sarah (1865–1913) 73
Hamilton, James, 6th earl of Abercorn (*c*.1661–1734) 15
Hamilton, Lady Mary (*fl.* 1731) 15
Haughey, Charles J. (1925–2006) 78
Hemmingway, Mary (*fl.* 1871) 65
Henry VIII, king (1491–1547) 11, 12
Hevey, G. (*fl.* 1825) 84
Hewson, Francis (1806–91) 54
Hickson, Gordon (*c*.1920–2015) 77
Highfield, Co. Kildare 8, 59, 60, 86
Hill, Arthur, 2nd marquess of Downshire (1753–1801) 12
Hill, Arthur, 3rd marquess of Downshire (1788–1845) 53
Hill, Henry (*fl.* 1955) 77
Hill, Maria (1815–) 59
Hogan, Garrett (*fl.* 1753) 16
Holt family 8, 26, 45, 46, 49, 59, 61, 62, 63, 74, 79
Holt, Alice (1793–1874) 60
Holt, Ann, née Grattan (1784–1853) 59
Holt, George (1759–1824) 44–5
Holt, John (1720–1804) 44–5
Holt, John (1795–1881) 45
Holt, John (1878–1925) 45, 74
Holt, Pearl (1932–) 77, 78
Holt, Samuel (1758–1848) 45, 62
Holt, Samuel (*c*.1786–1856) 45
Holt, Samuel (1821–1896) 64–5
Holt, Samuel (1840–1919) 45
Holt, Samuel John (1926–2019) 45, 77–78
Holt, Thomas (*fl.* 1801) 44

Hort, Josiah, archbishop of Tuam (c.1674–1751) 30, 41
Hurst family 58
Hurst, Elias (fl. 1689) 22
Hurst, Henry (fl. 1719) 22

Incorporated Society 23, 24, 25
Irish Church Act, 1869 69
Irish Countrywomen's Association 78
Irish Farmers' Association 60, 77, 78
Irish Land Commission 67, 75, 76
Irish Parliamentary Party 71
Irish Republican Army 71, 72, 73
Irish Transport and General Workers' Union 73
Irish Volunteers 71

Jackson family 24, 32
Jackson, wife of John (fl. 1772) 24
Jackson, Daniel (fl. 1853) 57–8
Jackson, John (fl. 1772) 24
Jackson, John (fl. 1798) 25, 38
Jackson, Thomas (fl. 1710) 31
Jackson, Thomas (1710–) 32
Jackson, William (fl. 1853) 57–8
Jackson, William (fl. 1888) 67
James II, king (1633–1701) 13, 28
Jellett, Anna Maria (1834–1909) 59
Johnstown, Co. Kildare 65
Johnstown Bridge, Co. Kildare 37, 39, 40, 52

Keegan, J. (fl. 1919) 74
Kelly, Denis (fl. 1737) 9
Kenny, Edward (fl. 1853) 85
Kildare Place Society 49–50, 51
Kilglass, Co. Kildare 11, 13, 37, 41–2
Kill, Co. Kildare 48
Killashee, Co. Kildare 48–9
Killaskillen, Co. Meath 28–9
Killinagh, Co. Kildare 11
Kilmore, Co. Kildare 11, 21, 32, 59
Kilrainy, Co. Kildare 30
Kilrathmurry, Co. Kildare 18
KIlshanroe, Co. Kildare 52
King, Sir John (c.1560–1637) 13
Kinnafad, Co. Kildare 11, 27, 30, 39
Kinnegad, Co. Westmeath 31
Kishavanna, Co. Kildare 11, 20, 22, 26, 46, 58, 85

Land Act, 1870 64, 65
Land Act, 1881 67
Land Act, 1885 67
Land Act, 1903 67, 68, 71, 76

Land Act, 1923 76
Land League 66, 67
Langan, Michael (fl. 1869) 62–3
Laois, county 31, 46
Leeson, Joseph, 4th earl of Milltown (1799–1866) 83
Limerick, county 14
Lindsay, Charles, bishop of Kildare (1760–1846) 48–50
Logan, Elizabeth (fl. 1810) 9
London, England 15, 23, 31, 35
Longford, county 43
Longridge, Co. Kildare 14, 58
Longwood, Co. Meath 82
Louth, county 28

McCann, James (fl. 1853) 58
McCann, Patrick (fl. 1744) 58
McCann, Richard (fl. 1853) 58
Macra na Feirme 77
McCrea, Joseph (c.1848–) 67–8
McKenny, Ellen (c.1818–) 84
McKenzy, Ellen (fl. 1846) 48
McKenny, Hannah (fl. 1818) 84
McKenny, Robert (fl. 1818) 84
McMahon, J. (fl. 1955) 77
Mallowny, Catherine (fl. 1713) 83
Mallowny, Charles (–1723) 83
Malta 43
Martin, Laurence (fl. 1830) 62
Martin, Thomas (fl. 1832) 62
Martinstown, Co. Kildare 27
Mather, Ada, née Bor (c.1860–1933) 72
Mather, Edward (1845–1898) 72
Mather, Harriet, née Tyrrell (1882–1969) 72
Mather, Henry (fl. 1777) 38
Mather, Henry (c.1789–1882) 65–6
Mather, Henry (c.1822–1901) 68
Mather, John (c.1827–99) 57
Mather, Thomas (fl. 1853) 57–8
Mather, Willa (1917–2007) 72
Mather, William (1888–1916) 72
Meath, county 15, 28, 31, 60, 73, 82
Medcalf, Alice, née Barcroft (1684–1732) 40–1
Medcalf, Joseph (1664–1737) 40–1
Metcalf, alias Medcalf, Joseph (1664–1737) 40–1
Metcalf, Francis (1797–1871) 86
Metcalf, George (fl. 1871) 65
Metcalf Park, Co. Kildare 13
Midland and Great Western Railway 56
Mills, Deborah (fl. 1722) 31
Mills, James (fl. 1703) 83

Moore, Henry, 1st earl of Drogheda (−1676) 14

Moore, James (*fl. c.*1744) 19

Moore, Lewis (*fl.* 1714) 37

Moran, Nick (*fl.* 1770) 83−4

More O'Ferrall family 8, 9, 56

More O'Ferrall, Ambrose (1752−1835) 43

More O'Ferrall, Letitia (−1859) 43

More O'Ferrall (née O'Ferrall), Richard (−1790) 28

More O'Ferrall, Richard (1797−1880) 9, 43

Motley, Thomas (*fl.* 1718) 30

Mountmellick, Co. Laois 49

Mountrath, Co. Laois 16

Moyfenrath, Upper, Co. Meath 73

Mullowney, Andrew (*fl.* 1805) 59

Mulrany, Patrick (*c.*1880−) 74−5

Murphy, Arthur (*fl.* 1881) 66

Murphy, James (*fl.*1847) 54

Murphy, William (*fl.* 1853) 58

Murphy, William (*fl.* 1881) 66

Napoleonic Wars 37

National Board for Education 50−1

National Farmers' Association 77−8

National League 67−8

Neill, William (*fl.* 1744) 22

Newberry Hall, Carbury, Co. Kildare 13, 17, 18, 23, 25, 27, 44, 54, 57, 64−5, 70

New Zealand 68

Nicolls, George A. (*c.*1817−84) 65

O'Brien, Thomas (*fl.* 1853) 85

O'Connor family 11

O'Ferrall, Richard (−1790) 28

Oldcourt, Co. Kildare 22, 24, 27, 57

O'More, Lewis (*fl.* 1641) 28

O'More, Rory (*fl.* 1641) 28

Palmer family 7, 28−30, 42, 43, 44, 56, 65, 69, 74−75

Palmer, Ann (*fl.* 1742)

Palmer, Charles (1731−1806) 28, 29, 30

Palmer, Charles (−1840) 25, 30

Palmer, Charles Colley (1845−1927) 30, 71, 74, 75

Palmer, Dudley (*fl.* 1742) 29

Palmer, George (*fl.* 1770) 29

Palmer, John (*fl.* 1742) 29

Palmer, Judith (*fl.* 1742) 29

Palmer, John (*fl. c.*1730) 29

Palmer, Margaret (*fl.* 1742) 29

Palmer, Mary (*fl.* 1742) 29

Palmer, Mary, née Colley (*fl.* 1708) 28−9

Palmer, Susanna (*fl.* 1742) 29

Palmer, Thomas (−1750) 28−9

Parsonstown, Co. Kildare 27, 40−1

Payne family 58

Payne, Charles (*c.*1810−) 69, 85

Payne, Charles (1853−) 69

Payne, John (*fl.* 1744) 19, 58

Payne, Joseph (*fl.* 1853) 85

Penn, William (1644−1718) 32

Phelan, James (*c.*1802−57) 54

Phillips, Matilda (*c.*1822−1892) 48

Pilkington, Frederick (*c.*1819−1898) 64−5

Pollard, J. (*fl.* 1955) 77

Pomeroy, Arthur, 1st Viscount Harberton (1723−98) 17, 23, 24, 44

Pomeroy, Arthur James, 3rd Viscount Harberton (1753−1832)

Pomeroy, Henry, 2nd Viscount Harberton (1749−1829) 25, 44

Pomeroy, James Spencer, 6th Viscount Harberton (1836−1912) 67−8

Pomeroy, John, 4th Viscount Harberton (1758−1833) 23

Pomeroy, John James, 5th Viscount Harberton (1790−1862) 53, 57, 64, 65

Pomeroy, Mary, née Colley, Viscountess Harberton (*fl.* 1764) 18, 23

Portlaoise, Co. Laois 78

Posseckstown, Co. Meath 60

Potterton family 60, 61, 79

Potterton, Godfrey(1956−) 60

Potterton, Hubert (1900−82) 77, 79

Potterton, Kenneth (1910−1996) 77

Potterton, Richard William (1820−82) 60

Potterton, Richard William (1859−1927) 60

Potterton, Thomas (1856−1921) 60, 79

Potterton, Thomas Edward (1896−1960) 60

Rahan, Co. Kildare 7, 13, 28, 29−30, 39, 44, 69, 74−5, 87

Rathcormick, Co. Meath 60

Rawson, Robert (*fl.* 1845) 85

Redmond, John (1856−1918) 71

Religious Sisters of Charity 43

Religious Society of Friends 31

Restoration 13, 14

Richmond, William (*fl.* 1908) 49

Rinaghan, Co. Kildare 21, 27

Robertstown, Co. Kildare 46, 86

Robins, John (1862−1942) 74,

Rocque, John (*c.*1704−62) 16

Roman Catholic Church 12, 46, 50, 51, 52

Roscommon, county 13, 35

Royal Canal 39

Royal Dublin Society 38
Royal Irish Constabulary 73

St Joseph's Orphanage, Co. Cavan 75
Sale family 34, 58, 60, 61, 79, 83
Sale, Alice, née Holt (1793–1874) 60
Sale, Martha (1823–80) 60
Sale, Samuel (*fl.* 1744) 20, 58
Sale, Samuel (1821–72) 58
Sale, Thomas (1792–1880) 57–8, 60
Sale, Thomas (*c.*1846–1917) 67
Sale, William (*c.*1842–91) 67
Salmon, Ann (*fl.* 1719) 22
Salmon, Henry (*fl.* 1691) 14, 22
Salmon, John (*fl.* 1719) 22
Scotland 11–12, 68
Scott, Jonathan (1668–1749) 20
Scully, Hugh (*fl.* 1719) 22
Second World War 77
1798 rebellion 24–6, 43, 44, 68
1641 rebellion 13, 28
Smith, Ann (*fl.* 1732) 32
Smith, Arthur (*fl.* 1798) 25
Smith, Arthur (*c.*1818–93) 66
Smith, Charles (–1890) 86
Smith, Jane (1790–1872) 86
Smith, Joan (1922–96) 77
Smith, John (*c.*1780–1843) 86
Smith, John (*fl.* 1853) 57–8
Smith, Judith (–*c.*1734) 32
Smith, William (*fl.* 1710) 31, 32
Smith, William (*fl.* 1798) 25
Smith, William (*c.* 1848–1909) 68
Smith, William R. (*fl.* 1888) 67
South Africa 68
Sparks, Stephen (*fl.* 1798) 24, 25
Spring, Thomas (*c.*1826–1903) 48
Stevenson, widow (*fl.* 1744) 20
Stonyhurst College, England 43
Strabane, Co. Tyrone 15
Stradbally, Co. Laois 18
Stronge, Robert (*c.*1820–1905) 63
Summerhill, Co. Meath 18

Tanderagee, Co. Kildare 19
Taylor, Alexander (1746–1828) 27, 37, 39
Twiss, Richard (1747–1821) 36

Tyrrell family 7, 25, 29, 33, 34, 61, 72
Tyrrell, Arthur (1929–2000) 79
Tyrrell, Edward (1873–1964) 74
Tyrrell, Francis (1926–2013) 77
Tyrrell, Garrett (1744–1805) 25
Tyrrell, Garrett (1851–1912) 66
Tyrrell, George (*fl.* 1771) 24
Tyrrell, Gerald (*fl. c.*1180) 7
Tyrrell, Harriet (1882–1969) 72
Tyrrell, Sir Hugh (–1199) 7
Tyrrell, Sir John (*fl. c.*1460) 7
Tyrrell, Joseph (1746–) 34
Tyrrell, Lizzie (*fl.* 1876) 63
Tyrrell, Robert (1905–93) 7
Tyrrell, Thomas (1690–1777) 34
Tyrrell, Thomas (1750–1811) 25, 34
Tyrrell, Thomas (1810–97) 85
Tyrrell, Thomas (1923–2008) 77
Tyrrell, William (–1748) 30
Tyrrell, William (1748–1803) 34
Tyrrell, William J.H. (1852–1933) 66, 70, 72–3
Tyrrell, William Upton (1896–1979) 72

United States of America 64, 68, 69
Upper Moyfenrath, Co. Meath 73
Ussher, Mary (*fl.* 1731) 19

Wales 35
Walsh, James (*fl.* 1853) 57–8
War of Independence 72–3
Waters, William (1828–1903) 56
Wellesley, Arthur, 1st duke of Wellington (1769–1852) 82
Wesley family 15
Wesley, Garret (–1728) 15
Wesley, Richard, né Colley (*c.*1690–1758) 15
Westmeath, county 73
Wicklow, county 47
William III, king (1650–1702) 13
Williamite war 28, 31
Williams, Adam (*fl.* 1777) 41
Williamstown, Co. Kildare 41, 48
Windmill, Co. Kildare 21, 37
Wodsworth, William D. (*c.*1817–87) 47
Wolstenholme, Edward (1782–1862) 44, 54, 83
Wyer, John (*c.*1851–82) 66, 86